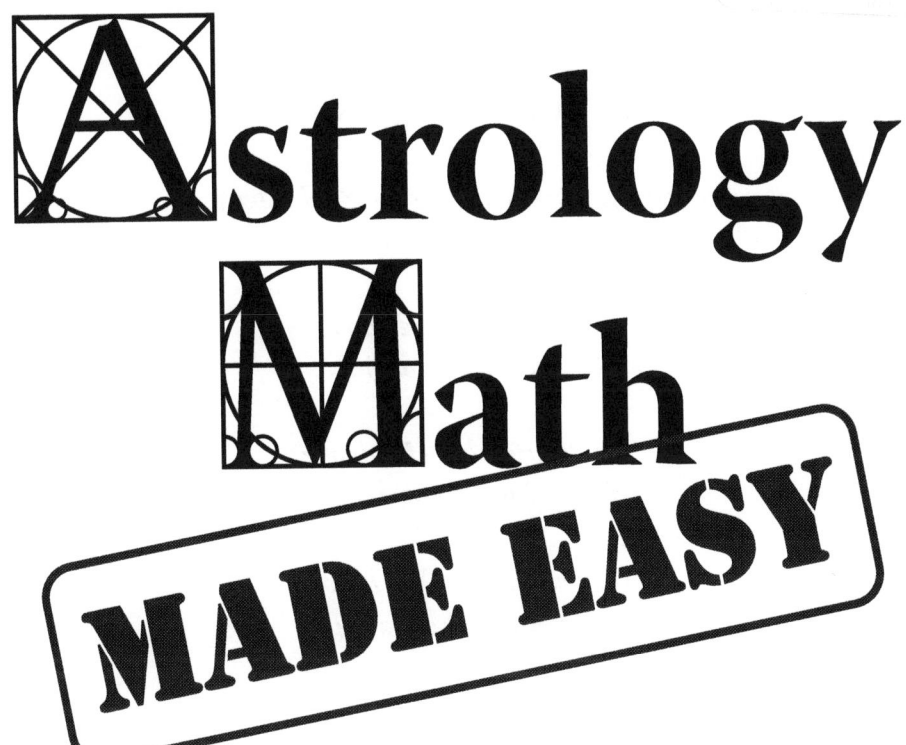

Other Books by Kevin B. Burk

Astrology: Understanding the Birth Chart
(Llewllyn, 2001)

The Complete Node Book
(Llewellyn, 2003)

The Relationship Handbook
(Serendipity Press, 2004)

The Relationship Workbook
(Serendipity Press, 2004)

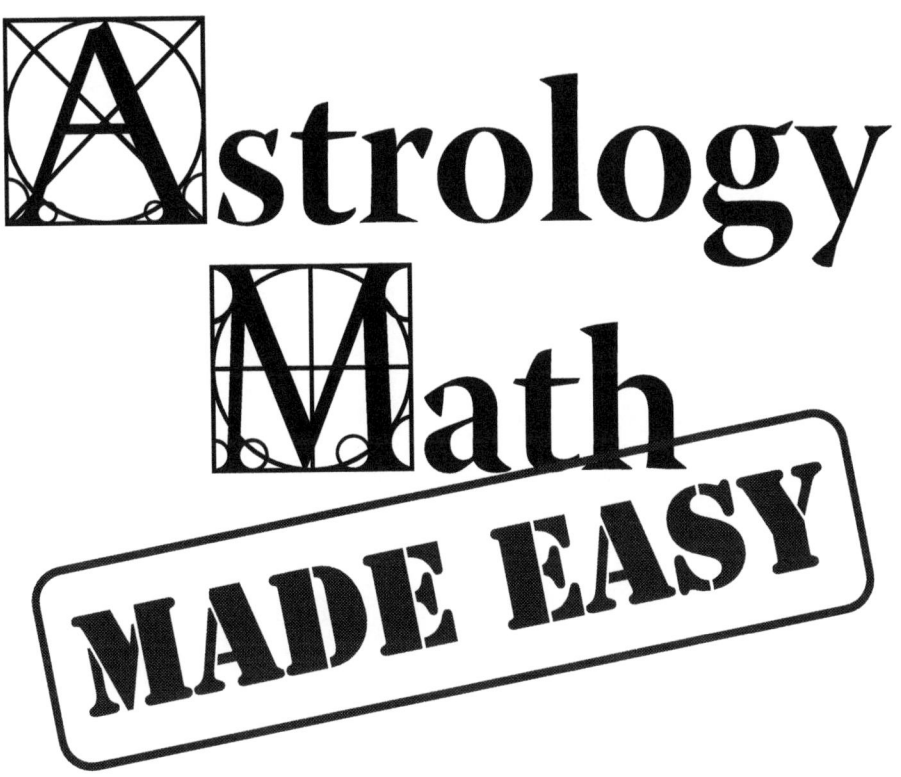

by

Kevin B. Burk

SAN DIEGO, CALIFORNIA

ISBN 0-9759682-4-6

©2005 Kevin B. Burk. All rights reserved. No part of this publication may be reproduced, transmitted, transcribed, stored in a retrieval system, or translated into any language, in any form, by any means, without written permission of the author.

Printed in the United States of America.

Published by
Serendipity Press
6161 El Cajon Blvd. #306
San Diego, CA 92115

All reference book tables are reproduced with permission from Astro Communications Services, Inc., P. O. Box 1646, El Cajon, CA 92022-1646 • 800-514-5070 (www.astrocom.com).

Book design and cover design by Kevin B. Burk.
Cover images ©2000 Visual Language®

Contents

Lesson 1:
Introduction to Astrology Math 1

So, Why Should I Bother to Learn the Math in the First Place?.................. 2
Exactly How Precise Should I Be? (Or, Why Don't My Charts Come Out Exactly Like My Computer Charts Do?)...................... 2
Converting Birth Time to Military Time 5

Lesson 2:
Time Conversions and Universal Time of Birth...5

Time and Date Conversions 5
Converting Birth Time from Military Time to Universal Time (UT) 6
Exercises 7

Lesson 3:
Longitude and Latitude Conversions and Calculations 9

Adding and Subtracting Degrees, Minutes and Seconds............................. 9
Adding Degrees, Minutes and Seconds................................. 9
Subtracting Degrees, Minutes and Seconds............................ 10
Converting to Smaller Units 11
Converting Units to Multiply and Divide............................... 11
Exercises Part 1: Adding and Subtracting 11
Converting to Larger Units in Decimal Form 12
Combining Up and Down Conversions 12
Converting Decimals back into Degrees, Minutes and Seconds 12
Exercises Part 2: Conversions 13

Lesson 4:
Interpolating the Planets 15

Calculating the Planet Travel Constant (PT) 16
Exercises Part 1: Calculate the PT for each of the following UTs 17
A Quick Look at the Ephemeris 17
Interpolating the Planets 1: Finding the Position of the Sun in the Birth Chart... 18
Interpolating the Planets 2: Finding the Position of the Moon in the Birth Chart 20
Interpolating the Planets 3: How to Interpolate Retrograde Planets 21
Interpolating the Planets 4: How to Interpolate Chiron Without a Daily Position 23

Contents (Continued)

Exercises Part 2: Calculate the PT and Interpolate the Birth Positions of the Following: 25

Lesson 5:
Finding the Sidereal Time of Birth 27

Some Definitions and Explanations Before We Proceed 28
Calculating the Sidereal Time of Birth 29
Sidereal Time in Eastern and Southern Hemisphere Charts 31
Exercises: Calculate the Sidereal Time 33

Lesson 6:
Interpolating the Angles and House Cusps 35

Finding the Sidereal Differential (SD) 36
Finding the Latitude Differential (LD) 37
Exercises Part 1: Find the SD and LD 38
Interpolating the Midheaven 39
Interpolating the Remaining House Cusps 40
IMPORTANT: This is Where Things Change!! 42
Exercises Part 2: Calculate the Remaining House Cusps 43
Interpolating the Cusps for Charts in Other Hemispheres 44
Exercises Part 3: Calculate the House Cusps for a Southern Hemisphere Chart 45
Exercises Part 4: Calculate and Draw Natal Charts 46

Lesson 7:
Relocation Charts 59

Calculating the Sidereal Time for the Relocated Chart 59
Exercises: Find the Relocated Sidereal Times 60

Lesson 8:
Solar and Lunar Return Charts 63

Solar Return Calculations 63
Finding the Universal Time (GMT) of the Return Chart 64
Lunar Return Calculations 64
The Synetic Vernal Point (SVP) 65
Exercises: Find the UT of the Return Charts 65
Precession Corrected Return Charts 65
Quarti-Returns and Demi-Returns 66

Contents (Continued)

Lesson 9:
Secondary Progressions 67

Finding the Progressed Dates in the Ephemeris 67
The Adjusted Calculation Date 68
Calculating the Progressed Planet Travel (PPT) Constant 68
Exercises: Calculate the PPT 71
Calculate the Solar Arc 71
Calculating the House Cusps—Three Different Methods 71
Solar Arc Directed Midheaven 72
Meridian Arc Directed Midheaven 73
Quotidian (Daily) Progressions 74

Lesson 10:
The Part of Fortune, the Vertex and the Equatorial Ascendant 77

Calculating the Part of Fortune (and the Part of Spirit) 77
Calculating the Vertex 78
Calculating the Equatorial Ascendant 79

Appendix A:
Answers to Exercises A-1

Lesson 2: Find the Universal Time and Date of Birth A-1
Lesson 3: Longitude and Latitude Conversions and Calculations A-1
Lesson 4: Interpolating the Planets A-2
Lesson 5: Finding the Sidereal Time of Birth A-3
Lesson 6: Interpolating the Angles and House Cusps A-4
Lesson 7: Relocated Charts A-18
Lesson 8: Find the UT of the Return Charts A-18
Lesson 9: Calculate the PPT A-19

Appendix B:
Astrology Math Formulas B-1

Converting From Standard Clock Time to Military Time B-1
Calculating the UT of Birth B-1
For Birth Locations West of Greenwich B-1
For Birth Locations East of Greenwich B-1
Calculating the Planet Travel (PT) Constant to Interpolate Planets B-1

Contents (Continued)

Calculating the Sidereal Time of Birth B-1
Calculating the Sidereal Time for Relocated Charts B-3
Calculating the Progressed Planet Travel (PPT) Constant B-4
Finding the Adjusted Calculation Date for Secondary
    Progressions B-4
Calculating Precession for Return Charts B-4
Calculating the Vertex B-4
Calculating the Equatorial Ascendant B-4

Appendix C:
Natal Chart Calculation Worksheet C-1

Lesson 1:
Introduction to Astrology Math

This workbook is designed to help you to overcome your fears about astrology math. If you didn't have at least some fears about learning how to calculate charts by hand, you wouldn't be reading this book. This is nothing to be ashamed of. Unless you have kids in high school, the last time you were presented with an algebra problem was probably when *you* were in high school.

And face it: you probably hated it then, too.

I promise you that this will be much easier for you than it was in high school. For one thing, you're allowed (and even expected) to use a calculator here. Math is, in fact, your *friend*. Granted, it's the kind of friend that wakes you up in the middle of the night, raids your refrigerator and then passes out on your living room floor, but it's still your friend. And if you're serious about learning astrology, you do have to be able to do the math—or at the very least understand how the math is done.

This workbook includes all of the tables and information you will need to complete all of the examples and exercises. If you want to be able to practice on your own, you will need a few extra tools, which are available as part of the **Reference Book Package** from **Astro Communications Services** at http://www.astrocom.com, or by phone at (800) 514-5070:

❖ An **Ephemeris**, such as Neil F. Michelsen's *The American Ephemeris for the 20th Century*. The Ephemeris is a listing of the daily positions of all of the planets at either Noon or Midnight, Greenwich Mean Time. We'll be using Neil F. Michelsen's **Midnight Ephemeris**, published by Astro Communications Services.

❖ An **Atlas**, such as Thomas G. Shanks' *The American Atlas,* and *The International Atlas.* These Atlases are designed for astrologers, and include not only the Latitude and Longitude, but also accurate listings of the time zones and time changes for each location.

❖ A **Book of Tables** for whatever house system you choose. We'll be using the **Koch House System,** and *The Michelsen Book of Tables* (for the Northern Hemisphere) in this workbook.

You will also need:

- ❖ A calculator—nothing fancy is required. As long as it adds, subtracts, divides and multiplies, you'll be fine.
- ❖ A pad of scratch paper.
- ❖ A pencil (or, if you're feeling daring, a pen).
- ❖ A valium (optional).

So, Why Should I Bother to Learn the Math in the First Place?

This is actually an excellent question. Today, professional—and even amateur—astrologers rely on their computers and computer software to calculate and draw their charts. Even if you don't have astrology software, you can obtain accurate charts, atlas, and time zone information for free on the web. Why should you learn how to do the calculations by hand?

Well, leaving aside the possibility that you would find yourself sitting down with a client during a power blackout, leaving you without access to your computer, there is a good reason to learn how to calculate charts by hand. Astrology is, fundamentally, about math. Even though computers have made the math a less intrusive and obvious element of astrology, from Babylon, Egypt and Greece through the Middle Ages and the Renaissance, right up through, in fact, the early 1980's, if you were an Astrologer, you had to know how to do all of your calculations by hand.

And yes, it was a royal pain in the rear, and no, no one wants to go back to doing things that way.

But understanding how to calculate charts by hand—whether you do so or not—helps you to understand how everything fits together, in a sense. You get a more organic understanding of how the houses and house cusps change through the day, and at different locations.

And finally (and for many of you more to the point) all of the current professional astrology certification exams require that you be able to calculate charts by hand. So if it makes this process any easier, you can always comfort yourself with the knowledge that once you learn the math and pass the tests, you will probably never have to do any of the math by hand again.

Exactly How Precise Should I Be? (Or, Why Don't My Charts Come Out Exactly Like My Computer Charts Do?)

One thing to remember is that we will be working with some very precise numbers, and when we work with them, we'll be rounding them off, something that the computer doesn't have to do when it calculates charts for us. The chances are that the charts you calculate by hand won't exactly match the charts that come from a computer program. For the most part, we will be rounding the final positions of the planets, angles and house cusps to the nearest minute, and so long as your answer is within 5 minutes of arc for all planets except for the Moon, or 12 minutes of arc for the Moon and all house cusps and angles, you've done the calculations correctly. If your answer is off by more than this amount, check your work: You've probably made a miscalculation somewhere along the line.

When doing the exercises in this book, however, **your answers should match almost exactly,** since all calculations in the examples were done by hand (with a calculator, of course), following the same steps as you are being taught, not by computer.

Notes

Lesson 2: Time Conversions and Universal Time of Birth

We'll be working with a lot of different units of measurement—both in *time* (**hours**, **minutes**, **seconds**) and in *longitude* (**signs**, **degrees**, **minutes**, **seconds**). We will have to learn how to work with these different units of measurement, and learn how to convert back and forth between different units.

Time and Date Conversions

We'll start with the most familiar units: time. We will be concerned with the following units of time in astrology: **day**, **hour**, **minute**, and **second**. For the most part, we won't be worrying too much about the seconds, at least not when it comes to birth times.

Here's how these units relate to each other:

1 Day = 24 Hours
1 Hour = 60 Minutes
1 Minute = 60 Seconds

Times are usually represented as being separated by colons, starting with hours, then minutes and finally seconds. For example, 04:15:29 is read as 4 hours, 15 minutes and 29 seconds.

In astrology the first thing that we have to do is to convert all times of birth into **military time,** which uses a 24-hour clock, rather than a 12-hour clock with the A.M./P.M. designations.

Converting Birth Time to Military Time

- ❖ If the birth time is A.M. then simply remove the A.M., and add a "0" before the hour if it's before 10:00. For example, 9:45 A.M. is 09:45 in military time. 11:28 A.M. is 11:28 in military time.

- ❖ If the birth time is P.M. then add "12" to the hour. For example, 8:30 P.M. is 20:30 in military time.

- ❖ Midnight in military time is 00:00. For birth times between 12:00 A.M. and 12:59 A.M., subtract the 12. For example, 12:15 A.M. is 00:15 in military time.

Converting Birth Time from Military Time to Universal Time (UT)

Universal Time (UT) refers to the Standard time in Greenwich, England at the moment in question. All birth times have to be converted from **Local Time** to **Universal Time,** because the planetary positions listed in the Ephemeris are based on either Noon or Midnight **Greenwich Mean Time (GMT).** Unless the local time zone at birth was GMT, we will have to make some time zone adjustments in order to find the **Universal Time of Birth.**

This is where the **Atlas** comes in. Not only does the Atlas give us the latitude and longitude information that we're going to need shortly, but it also lets us know what **time changes** were in effect for a given date at a given location. **This is extremely important!** Changes to Daylight Savings Time weren't standardized until recently. Some cities don't observe Daylight Savings Time at all. In the 1940's much of the country observed "War Time," which was the same 1-hour offset as Daylight Savings Time, except it was observed year-round. We will cover how to use the time change tables in the atlas soon. For now, let's just look at how they work.

Time zone changes are usually made in 1-hour increments, based on the number of zones east or west of Greenwich. If the location is **west of Greenwich,** the time zone change is **added to the birth time** to come up with the **Universal Time.** If the location is **east of Greenwich,** the time zone adjustment is **subtracted from the birth time** to come up with the **Universal Time.** If, when you add the time change, the hours are greater than 24, subtract 24 from the total (1 day, remember?) and move the date forward (it was the next day in Greenwich).

For example, let's take a person born on December 21, 1971 at 4:20 A.M. in New York, NY. The time zone in effect on that date was Eastern Standard Time (EST) and the offset for EST is +5:00.

❶ Convert to **Military time:** 4:20 A.M. = 04:20
❷ *ADD* Time Zone Offset: + 5:00
❸ Universal Time of Birth: 09:20, December 21, 1971

Here's another example. I was born on October 24, 1967 at 9:47 P.M., Central Daylight Time (CDT) which also has an offset of +5:00. Let's find my **UT** of birth.

❶ Convert to **Military Time:** 9:47 P.M. = 21:47
❷ *ADD* Time Zone Offset: + 5:00
❸ **Universal Time of Birth:** 26:47
❹ Subtract 24 Hours and add 1 day for **UT:** 02:47, *October 25, 1967*

Lesson 2: Time Conversions

Let's take an example or two from the Eastern Hemisphere and calculate the UT for June 21, 1975 at 06:30 P.M. in West Berlin, Germany (–1:00).

❶ Convert to **Military Time**: 6:30 P.M. =   18:30
❷ *SUBTRACT* Time Zone Offset: – 1:00
❸ **Universal Time of Birth**:   17:30, June 21, 1975

Of course, sometimes we have to subtract more hours than we have, and then the UT is the day before—as in this example: a person born on April 14, 1962 at 3:45 A.M. in Beijing, China (–8:00 offset).

❶ Convert to **Military Time**: 3:45 A.M. =   03:45, April 14, 1962
❷ *SUBTRACT* Time Zone Offset: –8:00
❸ This won't work just yet—we can't subtract 8 from 3, right? So we have to **borrow a whole day** (24 hours) and **add it to the date of birth,** as follows:
❹ Revised Time of Birth: 27:45,   *April 13, 1962*
❺ SUBTRACT Time Zone Offset: –8:00
❻ **Universal Time of Birth**:   19:45,   April 13, 1962.

Do you see how 03:45 on April 14, 1962 is the same as 27:45 on April 13, 1962? Even though we'd never express a time and date in this way, sometimes we have to convert days back into hours in order to make the correct time calculations. The same thing applies if you need to borrow an hour and add 60 to the minutes in order to subtract the minute column, and if you need to borrow a minute and add 60 seconds to the seconds column in order to subtract the seconds.

Exercises

Find the **Universal Time** and Date of Birth for the following examples. (All Time Zone Offsets are provided). The correct answers are provided in Appendix A. Remember, *west* of Greenwich, you *add* the time zone offset; *east* of Greenwich, you *subtract*.

1. January 8, 1954, 4:28 P.M., San Diego, California
   (PST, 8:00 W)

2. September 24, 1976, 11:00 A.M., Minneapolis, MN
   (CDT, 5:00 W)

3. May 16, 1944, 2:30 P.M., Boise, Idaho
   (MWT, 6:00 W)

4. April 18, 1961, 12:02 A.M., Honolulu, Hawaii (AHST, 10:00 W)

5. November 12, 1954, 2:53 A.M., Osaka, Japan (JST, 9:00 E)

6. February 19, 1970, 10:42 P.M., Moscow, Russia (UZ2, 3:00 E)

7. June 4, 1981, 5:25 A.M., Adelaide, Australia (ACST, 9:30 E)

8. December 31, 1972, 11:45 P.M., Scottsdale, AZ (MST, 7:00 W)

9. October 19, 1960, 2:45 P.M., London, England (GMT, 0:00 W)

10. July 23, 1980, 6:30 A.M., Auckland, New Zealand (NZT, 12:00 E)

Lesson 3: Longitude and Latitude Conversions and Calculations

As we become a bit more familiar with the different units and conversions, we will be adding, subtracting, multiplying and dividing various combinations of **time**, **latitude**, **longitude**, and **arc** measurements. Here are the conversions and relationships we will be working with:

1 Sign = 30 degrees (30°)
1 Degree = 60 minutes (60′)
1 Minute = 60 Seconds (60″)

Adding and Subtracting Degrees, Minutes and Seconds

We'll begin with the easy part: adding and subtracting measurements. Addition and subtraction are easy because they don't require that the measurements be expressed as a single unit. We can easily add 12 degrees and 45 seconds, or subtract 6 minutes from 2 degrees 8 minutes. If we want to multiply or divide, however, we'll have to convert the units (which we'll get to shortly).

Adding Degrees, Minutes and Seconds

We'll start with addition. You add degrees, minutes and seconds the same way that you add any other collection of numbers: you group the numbers by similar units, and add each group to come up with a total. For example:

```
  3° 24′ 15″       3 degrees  24 minutes  15 seconds
+ 8° 12′ 20″       8 degrees  12 minutes  20 seconds
                  11 degrees  36 minutes  35 seconds
```

You see? It's very easy. The only thing we have to watch for is when one of the units gets too big and we have to make adjustments in the final answer, as in this example:

```
  9° 44′ 06″       9 degrees  44 minutes  06 seconds
+ 6° 32′ 40″       2 degrees  32 minutes  40 seconds
                  15 degrees  76 minutes  46 seconds
```

What's wrong with this answer? You can never have more than 60 minutes because 60 minutes is 1 degree. So we have to convert the answer by subtracting 60 minutes (1 degree) from the minutes column, and adding (carrying) that 1 degree to the degree column.

	15 degrees	76 minutes	46 seconds
	[+ 1 degree]	[– 60 minutes]	
	16 degrees	16 minutes	46 seconds

Sometimes, we have to carry several times, and just as in regular mathematics, you always start with the smallest units and work your way up. And if you end up with more than 30 degrees, you will simply move up to the next sign (as you can see in the following example).

26 ♍	52′ 31″	=	26 degrees	(Virgo)	52 minutes	31 seconds
+ 7°	22′ 50″	=	7 degrees		22 minutes	50 seconds
			33 degrees	(Virgo)	74 minutes	81 seconds
					[+1 minute]	[– 60 seconds]
			33 degrees	(Virgo)	75 minutes	21 seconds
			[+1 degree]		[–60 minutes]	
			34 degrees	(Virgo)	15 minutes	21 seconds
			[–30 degrees]	[+1 Sign]		
			4 degrees	Libra	15 minutes	21 seconds	[4 ♎ 15′21″]

Subtracting Degrees, Minutes and Seconds

Subtraction works in much the same way. Simply group the similar units and subtract the one from the other. For example:

23° 54′ 45″	23 degrees	54 minutes	45 seconds
– 8° 12′ 20″	8 degrees	12 minutes	20 seconds
	15 degrees	42 minutes	25 seconds

Sometimes we will have to subtract a larger number from a smaller number, and to do that, we'll need to borrow from the next greater unit. The only difference is that when we borrow 1 **degree** to add it to the **minutes**, we're adding 60 minutes; likewise, when we borrow 1 **minute** and add it to the **seconds**, we're adding 60 seconds. Here's an example:

16°14′ 06″	16 degrees	14 minutes	06 seconds	=	16 degrees	13 minutes	66 seconds
– 9° 12′ 54″	9 degrees	12 minutes	54 seconds	=	9 degrees	12 minutes	54 seconds
					7 degrees	1 minute	12 seconds

Occasionally, we will have to borrow 1 **sign** and add 30 **degrees** to the degree column in order to perform our calculations, as in this example:

Lesson 3: Longitude and Latitude Conversions

```
  02 ♋ 18'36"    = 32 degrees (Gemini)   18 minutes   36 seconds
− 27 ♊ 05'19"    = 27 degrees (Gemini)   05 minutes   19 seconds
                    5 degrees            13 minutes   17 seconds
```

Exercises Part 1: Adding and Subtracting

1. 2° 45' 16"
   +18° 12' 42"

2. 14° 16' 58"
   + 3° 52' 34"

3. 18♑ 35' 20"
   +24° 18' 32"

4. 27♓ 52' 43"
   +14° 31' 48"

5. 26° 52' 09"
   −18° 34' 03"

6. 19° 14' 56"
   − 3° 59' 02"

7. 24♏ 18' 49"
   −13♏ 41' 38"

8.   6♒ 19' 51"
   −22° 46' 59"

Converting Units to Multiply and Divide

Although it is quite permissible to add and subtract multiple units (so long as you keep like units with like), in order to multiply or divide, only a single, common unit can be used. Much of astrology math involves multiplying or dividing measurements by a **constant** to find the position of the planet or house cusp in question. In order to do this, we have to know how to convert the original measurements into different single units of measurement, expressed as a base-10 decimal number. And once we've made our calculations, we will also need to be able to convert the decimals back into the more familiar degrees, minutes and seconds.

Converting to Smaller Units

When converting to smaller units, such as converting degrees into minutes, or minutes into seconds, start with the largest (and therefore the left-most) unit, and multiply it by 60. Add this number to the next unit. If additional conversions are needed (i.e., converting degrees into seconds), take this new number, and multiply it by 60 and add it to the last number. For example:

a. Original Arc: 12°32'18" =   12 degrees   32 minutes   18 seconds

b. Degrees to Minutes: 12 degrees × 60 = 720 minutes

c. Add to Minutes: 720 minutes + 32 minutes = 752 minutes

d. New Arc in Minutes/Seconds: 752 minutes   18 seconds

e. Minutes to Seconds: 752 minutes × 60 = 45,120 seconds

f. Add to Seconds: 45,120 seconds + 18 seconds = 45,138 seconds

Converting to Larger Units in Decimal Form

Not only will we need to convert larger units to smaller units, but we will also have to convert smaller units to larger units (usually converting seconds of arc into minutes of arc). **When converting from smaller to larger, we start with the smallest (right-most) units, and divide them by 60.** The result will be a decimal, which is the smaller units expressed in terms of the next larger unit. If additional conversions are needed (i.e., converting seconds to degrees), take this new number and divide it by 60. The result will be another decimal, which you then add to the degrees for the final result. We'll take the same example as above, only this time we'll express it in terms of degrees, rather than seconds.

a. Original Arc: 12°32′18″ = 12 degrees 32 minutes 18 seconds
b. Seconds to Minutes: 12 degrees 32 minutes [18 seconds ÷ 60 = 0.3 Min]
c. Add to Minutes: 12 degrees 32 minutes + 0.3 minutes
d. New Arc in Minutes/Seconds: 12 degrees 32.3 minutes
e. Minutes to Degrees: 12 degrees [32.3 minutes ÷ 60 = 0.5383 degrees]
f. Add to Degrees: 12 degrees + 0.5383 degrees = 12.5383 degrees

Combining Up and Down Conversions

Just to round things out, we can also express a figure of degrees, minutes and seconds in terms of minutes. This, of course, requires that we **convert both up and down,** as in the next example.

a. Original Arc: 12°32′18″ = 12 degrees 32 minutes 18 seconds
b. Seconds to Minutes (Up): 12 degrees 32 minutes [18 seconds ÷ 60 = 0.3 Min]
c. Add to Minutes: 12 degrees 32 minutes + 0.3 minutes
d. New Arc in Minutes/Seconds: 12 degrees 32.3 minutes
e. Degrees to Minutes (Down): [12 degrees x 60 = 720 minutes] + 32.3 minutes
f. Add total Minutes: 720 minutes + 32.3 minutes = 752.3 minutes

Converting Decimals back into Degrees, Minutes and Seconds

Once we've converted the arcs into a single unit (usually minutes, although when we interpolate the Moon, we'll do so in terms of degrees) and performed some simple calculations, we'll come up with another number in decimal form, which we will then need to convert back into degrees, minutes and seconds of arc. We do this in much the same way as we converted the original number into decimal form. First, we subtract the whole number to the left of the decimal point and make note of it. This is the number of the largest unit (i.e., if the decimal is in terms of degrees, the whole number is the number of degrees; if the decimal is in terms of minutes, the whole number is the number of minutes of arc).

Lesson 3: Longitude and Latitude Conversions

Multiplying the remainder (the decimal value) by 60 converts it to the next smaller unit (minutes or seconds of arc). Again, we subtract the whole number before the decimal point and make note of it. If we're converting from degrees, we'll do this one more time, and multiply this new remainder by 60, rounding the result to the nearest whole number to find the value for the seconds of arc.

It's nowhere near as confusing as it seems. We'll use the same example we've been using and convert 12.5383 degrees back into degrees, minutes and seconds.

a. Decimal Value: 12.5383 degrees

b. Subtract Whole Number: 12 degrees + 0.5383 degrees

c. Convert decimal to Minutes: 12 degrees + [0.5383 degrees x 60 = 32.298 Min.]

d. Subtract Whole Number: 12 degrees 32 minutes + 0.298 minutes

e. Convert decimal to Seconds: 12 degrees 32 minutes + [0.298 Min x 60 = 17.88 Sec.]

f. Round Seconds off: 12 degrees 32 minutes 18 seconds

Exercises Part 2: Conversions

9. Convert 18°36′49″ to degrees.

10. Convert 2°10′15″ to seconds.

11. Convert 5°48′32″ to minutes.

12. Convert 52′16″ to minutes.

13. Convert 11°48′21″ to degrees.

14. Convert 8°16′29″ to minutes.

15. Convert 24.8621° to degrees, minutes and seconds of arc.

16. Convert 19.0249° to degrees, minutes and seconds of arc.

17. Convert 48.6201′ to minutes and seconds of arc.

18. Convert 2.962′ to minutes and seconds of arc.

19. Convert 30.7334′ to minutes and seconds of arc.

20. Convert 9.2263° to degrees, minutes and seconds of arc.

Lesson 4: Interpolating the Planets

Now we'll start to apply some of what we've learned to calculate the positions of the planets in the natal chart. This process is called **interpolation**, and involves the simple application of ratios, proportions and percentages (which those of you with excellent memories may remember from your high school algebra classes).

We're working with three known quantities that relate to each other, and are looking for the fourth. What we know is the position of each planet at Midnight (**Universal Time**) on the date of birth; the position of each planet at Midnight (**Universal Time**) on the following day, and the **Universal Time of birth**. Right away, we can easily calculate how far the planet traveled in the 24-hour period by looking at the difference between the two positions as listed in the **Ephemeris**. So we know that on the date of birth, the planet was somewhere within that range of motion.

What we need to know, however, is exactly where the planet was at the time of birth. How far had it traveled from point A (Midnight on the date of birth) to point B (Midnight on the next day)? The ratio of the distance the planet travels from midnight on the date of birth to the **Universal Time** of birth (which we will call **ΔP**), to the total distance the planet will travel from midnight to midnight (which we we'll call **DT**) is the same as the ratio of the **Universal Time of Birth** (**UT**) to the 24-hour period. The formula looks something like this:

$$\frac{\Delta P}{DT} = \frac{UT}{24 \text{ Hrs}}$$

What we're looking for in this formula is **ΔP**, the distance the planet has traveled by the time of birth. We can find it by dividing the **Universal Time** by 24 hours to come up with a percentage (i.e., what percent of the day has completed at the **UT** of birth). We can then apply that same percentage to the **DT** (total distance traveled during the 24-hour period) and find the **ΔP**.

Let's take an easy example to illustrate how this works. If we know that the Sun traveled 1° during a 24-hour period, say from 1♍00 to 2♍00, if the **UT** of birth was, say 12:00 (which is exactly half of the 24-hour day), the sun will have traveled half of the total distance, or 30′ of arc. We add this travel distance (ΔP) to the original position of the Sun, and find that the Sun's position at the 12:00 noon UT of birth is 1♍30.

This works for any birth time (UT). In every case, what we need to discover is what percentage of the day that the birth time represents (25%? 37.63%?). Once we know that, we know what percentage of the total distance the planet has covered by that point in time. This percentage will be expressed as a decimal constant, that we will call the **Planet Travel Constant, or PT**. This is an extremely important number, as it applies to every single planet. Once you have calculated this number, write it down so you won't forget it! If you use the **Natal Chart Calculation Worksheet,** there is a space there for you to record the PT.

Here is a more graphic representation of what we're looking for:

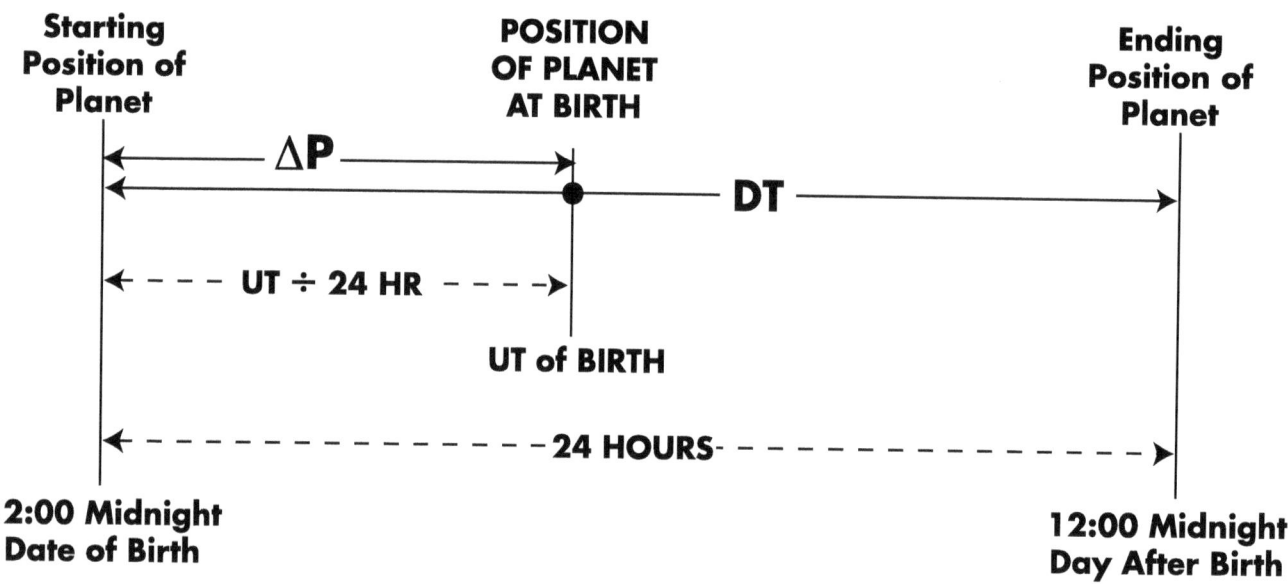

Calculating the Planet Travel Constant (PT)

In order to calculate the PT, we **divide the UT of birth by 24 hours.** Before we can do this, however, we have to express the UT of birth as hours only, rather than as hours and minutes. Any time we need to either multiply or divide two numbers, we have to make sure that we're comparing apples to apples, and that both numbers are in the same units.

Converting the UT to hours is very simple. **We simply take the minutes portion of the UT of birth, and divide it by 60** (because there are 60 minutes in an hour). The answer will be a decimal value less than 1.0 (because there aren't enough minutes to make up a full hour). We add the hours portion of the UT to this decimal, and we have the UT of birth expressed in hours, and can now divide this number by 24 hours to come up with the PT decimal.

NOTE: All calculations can be rounded to four decimal places.

Lesson 4: Interpolating the Planets

Here's an example, using my own **UT** of birth, 02:47.

a.	UT of Birth	02 hours	47 minutes
b.	Convert minutes		47 minutes ÷ 60 = 0.7833
c.	UT of Birth in Hours:		2 hours + 0.7833 minutes = 2.7833 hours
d.	Divide by 24 Hrs to find PT:		2.78333 ÷ 24 = 0.116
e.	PT Decimal is 0.116.		

To interpolate the positions of the planets in my chart, then, we simply multiply the total distance traveled by the **PT** of 0.116, and add the answer to the original position of the planet (or, if the planet is in retrograde motion, subtract this answer from the planet's original position).

Exercises Part 1: Calculate the PT for each of the following UTs

1. 06:42
2. 20:15
3. 16:50
4. 08:22
5. 22:30

A Quick Look at the Ephemeris

The **ephemeris**, as we've already explained, is a book that lists the daily positions of the planets for a given time and location. Most ephemerides use Greenwich, England as the location, and either 12:00 noon or 12:00 midnight GMT as the reference time. On the following page is an example of the planetary positions for October, 1967, taken from *The American Ephemeris for the 20th Century (Midnight)* by Neil F. Michelsen, published by ACS Publications.

We will pull a great deal of information from the Ephemeris in our calculations. For now, simply familiarize yourself with the way the information is laid out. The dates are listed down the leftmost column, followed by the **Midnight Sidereal Time** (which we will need in the next lesson), and then by each of the planets in turn, including the North Node of the Moon. **Retrograde** planets are indicated by an "R" after the degrees, and planets in retrograde motion are shaded gray until they once again turn **direct** (indicated by a "D"). In the above example, Mercury turned retrograde on the 21st of October, and Saturn is retrograde the entire month.

LONGITUDE — OCTOBER 1967

Day	Sid.Time	☉	0 hr ☽	Noon ☽	True ☊	☿	♀	♂	♃	♄	♅	♆	♇
1 Su	0 36 9	7♎ 7 40	27♌49 46	5♍ 1 21	28♈ 3.0	1♏10.2	29♌42.6	14♐10.2	26♌42.7	9♈10.0	25♍36.6	22♏27.5	21♍ 3.6
2 M	0 40 6	8 6 41	12♍18 52	19 41 37	28R 0.2	2 24.4	0♍ 5.9	14 52.1	26 54.1	9R 5.3	25 40.3	22 29.2	21 5.7
3 Tu	0 44 3	9 5 45	27 8 46	4♎39 18	27 57.9	3 37.1	0 30.9	15 34.2	27 5.4	9 0.6	25 44.0	22 31.0	21 7.8
4 W	0 47 59	10 4 50	12♎12 9	19 46 7	27 56.5	4 48.2	0 57.7	16 16.3	27 16.7	8 55.8	25 47.7	22 32.7	21 9.9
5 Th	0 51 56	11 3 57	27 20 4	4♏52 50	27D 56.0	5 57.4	1 26.0	16 58.6	27 27.9	8 51.1	25 51.4	22 34.5	21 12.0
6 F	0 55 52	12 3 7	12♏23 21	19 50 38	27 56.3	7 4.7	1 55.9	17 41.0	27 39.0	8 46.4	25 55.1	22 36.3	21 14.0
7 Sa	0 59 49	13 2 18	27 13 52	4♐32 20	27 57.2	8 10.0	2 27.3	18 23.5	27 50.0	8 41.7	25 58.8	22 38.1	21 16.1
8 Su	1 3 45	14 1 31	11♐45 32	18 53 4	27 58.4	9 12.9	3 0.2	19 6.0	28 0.9	8 37.0	26 2.4	22 40.0	21 18.2
9 M	1 7 42	15 0 46	25 54 44	2♑50 26	27 59.3	10 13.5	3 34.4	19 48.7	28 11.8	8 32.4	26 6.1	22 41.8	21 20.2
10 Tu	1 11 38	16 0 3	9♑40 12	16 24 11	27R 59.9	11 11.4	4 10.0	20 31.5	28 22.5	8 27.7	26 9.7	22 43.7	21 22.3
11 W	1 15 35	16 59 22	23 2 34	29 35 38	27 59.9	12 6.4	4 46.9	21 14.4	28 33.2	8 23.1	26 13.3	22 45.6	21 24.3
12 Th	1 19 32	17 58 42	6♒ 3 43	12♒27 9	27 59.4	12 58.2	5 25.1	21 57.4	28 43.8	8 18.4	26 16.9	22 47.5	21 26.3
13 F	1 23 28	18 58 4	18 46 18	25 1 33	27 58.5	13 46.6	6 4.4	22 40.4	28 54.4	8 13.8	26 20.5	22 49.4	21 28.3
14 Sa	1 27 25	19 57 28	1♓13 15	7♓21 46	27 57.4	14 31.1	6 44.9	23 23.6	29 4.8	8 9.3	26 24.1	22 51.4	21 30.3
15 Su	1 31 21	20 56 53	13 27 28	19 30 40	27 56.3	15 11.5	7 26.6	24 6.8	29 15.1	8 4.7	26 27.6	22 53.4	21 32.2
16 M	1 35 18	21 56 20	25 31 42	1♈30 50	27 55.5	15 47.2	8 9.3	24 50.2	29 25.4	8 0.2	26 31.1	22 55.3	21 34.2
17 Tu	1 39 14	22 55 50	7♈28 24	13 24 40	27 54.9	16 17.9	8 53.1	25 33.6	29 35.5	7 55.7	26 34.6	22 57.3	21 36.1
18 W	1 43 11	23 55 21	19 19 53	25 14 20	27D 54.6	16 43.1	9 37.9	26 17.1	29 45.6	7 51.3	26 38.1	22 59.3	21 38.0
19 Th	1 47 7	24 54 54	1♉ 8 18	7♉ 2 2	27 54.6	17 2.3	10 23.7	27 0.7	29 55.5	7 46.9	26 41.6	23 1.4	21 39.9
20 F	1 51 4	25 54 29	12 55 49	18 49 57	27 54.6	17 14.9	11 10.4	27 44.4	0♍ 5.4	7 42.5	26 45.0	23 3.4	21 41.8
21 Sa	1 55 1	26 54 7	24 44 45	0♊40 33	27 54.8	17R 20.3	11 58.0	28 28.1	0 15.2	7 38.2	26 48.4	23 5.5	21 43.7
22 Su	1 58 57	27 53 46	6♊37 41	12 36 33	27R 54.8	17 18.1	12 46.5	29 12.0	0 24.8	7 33.9	26 51.8	23 7.5	21 45.6
23 M	2 2 54	28 53 28	18 37 31	24 41 2	27 54.8	17 7.7	13 35.9	29 55.9	0 34.4	7 29.7	26 55.2	23 9.6	21 47.4
24 Tu	2 6 50	29 53 12	0♋47 32	6♋55 28	27 54.6	16 48.6	14 26.1	0♑39.9	0 43.8	7 25.5	26 58.5	23 11.7	21 49.2
25 W	2 10 47	0♏52 58	13 11 18	19 29 30	27 54.4	16 20.7	15 17.0	1 24.0	0 53.2	7 21.4	27 1.8	23 13.8	21 51.0
26 Th	2 14 43	1 52 47	25 52 33	2♌20 52	27D 54.2	15 43.7	16 8.7	2 8.2	1 2.4	7 17.3	27 5.1	23 15.9	21 52.8
27 F	2 18 40	2 52 38	8♌54 53	15 34 56	27 54.2	14 57.7	17 1.2	2 52.4	1 11.5	7 13.3	27 8.4	23 18.1	21 54.6
28 Sa	2 22 36	3 52 30	22 21 18	29 14 12	27 54.5	14 3.2	17 54.3	3 36.7	1 20.6	7 9.4	27 11.6	23 20.2	21 56.3
29 Su	2 26 33	4 52 25	6♍13 41	13♍19 42	27 55.0	13 0.9	18 48.1	4 21.1	1 29.5	7 5.5	27 14.8	23 22.4	21 58.0
30 M	2 30 30	5 52 23	20 32 20	27 50 20	27 55.7	11 52.0	19 42.6	5 5.6	1 38.2	7 1.6	27 18.0	23 24.5	21 59.7
31 Tu	2 34 26	6 52 23	5♎14 2	12♎42 24	27 56.4	10 38.1	20 37.7	5 50.2	1 46.9	6 57.9	27 21.2	23 26.7	22 1.4

Astro Data Dy Hr Mn	Planet Ingress Dy Hr Mn	Last Aspect Dy Hr Mn	☽ Ingress Dy Hr Mn	Last Aspect Dy Hr Mn	☽ Ingress Dy Hr Mn	☽ Phases & Eclipses Dy Hr Mn	Astro Data 1 OCTOBER 1967
☽ O S 3 12:13	♀ ♍ 1 18:07	1 3:14 ♀ ♂	♍ 1 3:38	31 2:47 ♄ ☍	♏ 1 15:26	3 20:24 ● 9♎56	Julian Day # 24745
☽ O N 16 18:38	♃ ♍ 19 10:51	2 21:43 ♅ ♂	♎ 3 4:34	3 10:55 ♅ ⚹	♐ 3 14:51	10 12:11 ☽ 16♑30	Delta T 38.1 sec
♄ ♇ ⚷ 16 18:07	♂ ♐ 23 2:14	5 0:13 ♆ ⚹	♏ 5 4:14	5 11:47 ♅ □	♑ 5 15:44	18 10:11 ○ 24♈21	SVP 05♓42'45"
☿ R 21 5:15	☉ ♏ 24 2:44	7 1:00 ♃ □	♐ 7 4:32	7 16:09 ♃ △	♒ 7 19:45	18 10:15 ⚹T 1.143	Obliquity 23°26'45"
☽ O S 30 23:19		9 3:59 ♃ △	♑ 9 7:04	9 15:50 ♆ □	♓ 10 3:42	26 12:04 ☾ 2♌23	⚷ Chiron 27♓05.1R
☿ D 10 16:16	♀ ♎ 9 16:32	11 5:50 ♅ △	♒ 11 12:45	12 10:52 ♃ ☍	♈ 12 14:58		☽ Mean ☊ 28♈51.8
♀ O S 12 3:36	☉ ♐ 23 0:04	13 19:47 ♃ ☍	♓ 13 21:38	14 10:05 ♂ □	♉ 15 3:52	2 5:48 ● 9♏07	1 NOVEMBER 1967
☽ O N 13 0:37		16 1:59 ♅ △	♈ 16 8:58	17 13:00 ♅ △	♊ 17 16:40	2 5:38:17 ⚹T non-C	Julian Day # 24776
♄ O S 18 9:03		18 21:30 ♃ △	♉ 18 21:41	20 0:51 ♅ □	♋ 20 4:13	9 1:00 ☽ 15♒56	Delta T 38.1 sec
☽ O S 27 8:37		21 4:12 ♅ △	♊ 21 10:38	22 12:54 ☉ △	♌ 22 13:47	17 4:53 ○ 24♉09	SVP 05♓42'42"
		23 22:04 ☉ △	♋ 23 22:27	24 10:38 ♀ □	♍ 24 20:46	25 0:23 ☾ 2♍02	Obliquity 23°26'45"
		26 2:16 ♅ ⚹	♌ 26 7:40	26 22:20 ♅ ♂	♎ 27 0:48		⚷ Chiron 25♓52.6R
		28 1:44 ♆ □	♍ 28 13:19	28 22:37 ♂ □	♏ 29 2:13		☽ Mean ☊ 27♈13.3
		30 11:09 ♅ ♂	♎ 30 15:31				

Figure Copyright © 1994, Neil F. Michelsen

Interpolating the Planets 1:
Finding the Position of the Sun in the Birth Chart

Let's work through the first few planets in my chart, using the table from the **Natal Chart Calculation Worksheet** as examples. We've already calculated all of the necessary information, and I've filled in the Start and End positions of the Sun from the **Midnight Ephemeris**.

Universal Time (UT) of Birth: 02:47, October 25, 1967

Planet Travel (PT) (UT÷24 hrs): 0.116

Planet	Start	End	Total Travel	Travel × PT	Birth Position
☉	0♏52'58"	1♏52'47"			

Lesson 4: Interpolating the Planets

To find how far the Sun has traveled in this 24-hour period, we subtract the Start position on October 25, from the End position on October 26. Note how we have to both borrow 60 seconds and 60 minutes in order to be able to subtract the one from the other.

$$1°♏52'47'' = 1°52'47'' = 1°51'107'' = 0°111'107''$$
$$-0°♏52'58'' = 0°52'58'' = 0°52'58'' = 0°52'58''$$
$$\phantom{-0°♏52'58'' = 0°52'58'' = 0°52'58'' = {}}0°59'49'' \text{ Total Travel}$$

We then need to convert the total travel time into a single unit in order to multiply it by the **PT**. For every planet except for the Moon (which covers roughly 12°–15° of arc each day), we will convert the **Total Travel** distance into minutes, by dividing the seconds by 60 and adding the result to the minutes.

a. Total Travel   59 Minutes   49 Seconds

b. Seconds ÷ 60   49 Seconds ÷ 60 = 0.8167 Minutes

c. Total Travel   59 Minutes + 0.8167 Minutes = 59.8167 Minutes

This is the number that we want to write in the "Total Travel" box.

Planet Travel (PT) (UT÷24 hrs)   0.116

Planet	Start	End	Total Travel	Travel x PT	Birth Position
☉	0♏52'58''	1♏52'47''	**59.8167'**		

Next, we multiply the total travel in minutes by the **PT** decimal to find Δ**P**.

$$59.8167' \times 0.116 = 6.9387'$$

Let's convert this back into minutes and seconds.

a. Minutes in Decimal Form: 6.9387 = 6 minutes + 0.9387 minutes

b. Decimal x 60 to find Seconds: 6 minutes + [0.9387 x 60] minutes = 56 seconds

c. ΔP in Minutes and Seconds: 6 minutes 56 seconds

Add this result to the table.

Planet Travel (PT) (UT÷24 hrs)   0.116

Planet	Start	End	Total Travel	Travel x PT	Birth Position
☉	0♏52'58''	1♏52'47''	59.8167'	**6'56''**	

Finally, since the Sun is (always) in direct motion, we add this amount to the original position of the Sun to find the Sun's position in the natal chart.

$$0♏52'58''$$
$$+\quad 06'56''$$
$$0♏58'114'' \quad = \quad 0♏59'54'' \quad = \quad 1♏00$$

Planet Travel (PT) (UT÷24 hrs)   0.116

Planet	Start	End	Total Travel	Travel x PT	Birth Position
☉	0♏52'58"	1♏52'47"	59.8167'	6'56"	1♏00

Interpolating the Planets 2: Finding the Position of the Moon in the Birth Chart

Finding the position of the Moon in the Birth Chart is exactly the same as finding the position of the Sun, except that since the Moon can cover between 12°–15° in a 24-hour period, we will be working in terms of *degrees*, rather than *minutes*. When taking the Moon's position from the Ephemeris, make sure that you take the **midnight position of the Moon** (from the first column, designated "0 hr"). Both the midnight and noon positions of the Moon are listed in the ephemeris because the Moon moves so quickly. Again, I've filled in the start and end positions for the Moon in my chart.

Planet Travel (PT) (UT÷24 hrs)   0.116

Planet	Start	End	Total Travel	Travel x PT	Birth Position
☉	0♏52'58"	1♏52'47"	59.8167'	6'56"	1♏00
☽	13♋11'18"	25♋52'33"			

As before, we'll subtract the start position from the end position to find the total travel, and then convert this result into degrees. In this example, we don't have to borrow or convert any of the numbers, and can easily subtract the one from the other.

$$25♋52'33'' \quad = \quad 25°52'33''$$
$$-\ 13♋11'18'' \quad = \quad 13°11'18''$$
$$12♋41'15'' \quad = \quad 12°41'15'' \text{ Total Travel}$$

We then convert this number to degrees as follows:

a. Total Travel   12 degrees   41 minutes   15 seconds
b. Convert Seconds   12 degrees   41 minutes   15 seconds ÷ 60 = 0.25 min.
c. Degrees and Minutes   12 degrees   41.25 minutes
d. Convert Minutes   12 degrees   41.25 minutes ÷ 60 = 0.6875 degrees
e. Total Travel Degrees 12 degrees + 0.6875 degrees = 12.6875 degrees

Planet Travel (PT) (UT÷24 hrs)   0.116

Planet	Start	End	Total Travel	Travel x PT	Birth Position
☉	0♏52'58"	1♏52'47"	59.8167'	6'56"	1♏00
☽	13♋11'18"	25♋52'33"	**12.6875°**		

Next, we multiply the total travel by the **PT**.

$$12.6875° \times 0.116 = 1.4718 \text{ degrees}$$

We convert this back into degrees, minutes and seconds as follows:

a. Degrees in Decimal Form: 1.4718 = 1 degree + 0.4718 minutes

b. Decimal x 60 to find Minutes: 1 degree + [0.4718 x 60] degrees = 28.31 minutes

c. Degrees and Minutes: 1 degree + 28 minutes + 0.31 minutes

d. Decimal x 60 to find Seconds 1 degree + 28 min + [0.31 x 60] min = 18 seconds

e. ΔP in Degree/Minute/Second: 1 degree 28 minutes 18 seconds [1°28'18"]

Planet Travel (PT) (UT÷24 hrs)   0.116

Planet	Start	End	Total Travel	Travel x PT	Birth Position
☉	0♏52'58"	1♏52'47"	59.8167'	6'56"	1♏00
☽	13♋11'18"	25♋52'33"	12.6875°	**1°28'18"**	

And finally, to find the birth position of the Moon, we add the **ΔP** to the start position of the Moon.

```
  13♋11'18"   =   13° 11' 18"
+  1  28'18"  =    1° 28' 18"
  ─────────       ──────────
  14♋39'36"   =   14♋39'36"   = 14♋39 Position of the Moon.
```

Planet Travel (PT) (UT÷24 hrs)   0.116

Planet	Start	End	Total Travel	Travel x PT	Birth Position
☉	0♏52'58"	1♏52'47"	59.8167'	6'56"	1♏00'
☽	13♋11'18"	25♋52'33"	12.6875°	1°28'18"	**14♋39**

Interpolating the Planets 3:
How to Interpolate Retrograde Planets

The next example we will address covers just about every other variable you will encounter from this point on. It will introduce you to how the rest of the planets appear in the Ephemeris, and it will also show you how to handle planets in **retrograde motion.** Conveniently enough, we can accomplish this simply by interpolating the position of Mercury in my birth chart. As before, I've filled in the start and end positions of Mercury in the table for you.

Planet Travel (PT) (UT÷24 hrs)   0.116

Planet	Start	End	Total Travel	Travel x PT	Birth Position
☉	0♏52'58"	1♏52'47"	59.8167'	6'56"	1♏00'
☽	13♋11'18"	25♋52'33"	12.6875°	1°28'18"	14♋39
☿	16♏20.7℞	15♏43.7℞			

The first thing that you may notice is that all of the rest of the planets from Mercury through Pluto have **already had the seconds converted into decimal form in terms of minutes,** so you won't have to perform this step again. Wasn't that thoughtful?

The next thing that you may notice is that the ending position for Mercury is earlier than the starting position for Mercury—this is, of course, because Mercury is in retrograde motion. In the ACS Ephemeris, retrograde planets are designated with gray shading in the table.

We still need to find the total travel distance for Mercury, but since Mercury is retrograde, we'll have to **subtract the *end* position from the *start* position,** instead of the other way around.

$$\begin{array}{rcccc} 16♏20.7 & = & 16°20.7 & = & 15°\ 80.7 \\ -\ 15♏43.7 & = & 15°43.7 & = & 15°\ 43.7 \\ \hline & & & & 0°\ 37\ \text{Total Travel} \end{array}$$

Since this number is already in minutes, we simply record it in the table and move on to the next step.

Planet Travel (PT) (UT÷24 hrs)   0.116

Planet	Start	End	Total Travel	Travel x PT	Birth Position
☉	0♏52'58"	1♏52'47"	59.8167'	6'56"	1♏00'
☽	13♋11'18"	25♋52'33"	12.6875°	1°28'18"	14♋39
☿	16♏20.7℞	15♏43.7℞	**37'**		

We find the **ΔP** by multiplying the 37 minutes of travel by the **PT**.

37 minutes x 0.116 = 4.292 minutes

Again, since the original positions of the planets are expressed in terms of degrees and minutes, we don't have to convert this number, and can enter it in the table as is.

Planet Travel (PT) (UT÷24 hrs)   0.116

Planet	Start	End	Total Travel	Travel x PT	Birth Position
☉	0♏52'58"	1♏52'47"	59.9167'	6'56"	1♏00'
☽	13♋11'18"	25♋52'33"	12.6875°	1°28'18"	14♋39
☿	16♏20.7℞	15♏43.7℞	37'	**4.292'**	

Now, because Mercury is Retrograde and therefore moving backwards, we will *subtract* the ΔP from the start position rather than adding it (because Mercury ends up at an earlier position in the birth chart, rather than a later one).

	16♏20.7	=	16°20.700
–	4.292	=	4.292
			16°16.408 = 16♏16℞ Mercury

Planet Travel (PT) (UT÷24 hrs) 0.116

Planet	Start	End	Total Travel	Travel x PT	Birth Position
☉	0♏52'58"	1♏52'47"	59.8167'	6'56"	1♏00'
☽	13♋11'18"	25♋52'33"	12.6875°	1°28'18"	14♋39
☿	16♏20.7℞	15♏43.7℞	37'	4.292'	**16♏16 ℞**

Interpolating the Planets 4: How to Interpolate Chiron Without a Daily Position

Unless you have an ephemeris that lists the daily positions of the asteroids, finding the position of Chiron in the birth chart is a slightly different process. The ACS Ephemeris lists the position of Chiron at Midnight on the first day of each month (in the "Astro Data" table at the bottom of each page—see the illustration below), but does not include Chiron's daily motion.

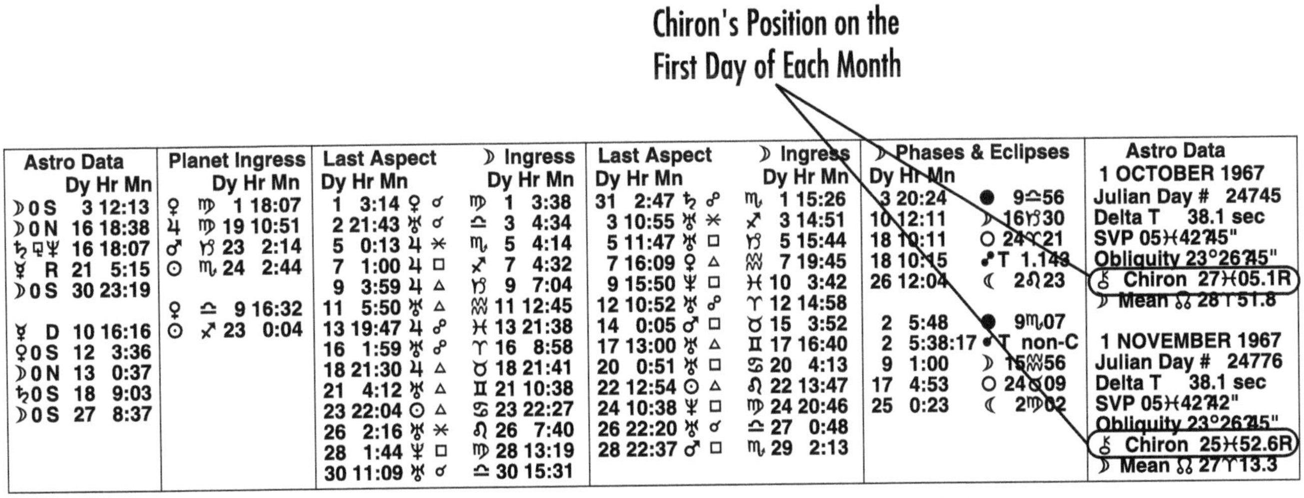

Chiron's Position on the First Day of Each Month

Astro Data	Planet Ingress	Last Aspect	☽ Ingress	Last Aspect	☽ Ingress	☽ Phases & Eclipses	Astro Data
Dy Hr Mn	Dy Hr Mn	Dy Hr Mn	Dy Hr Mn	Dy Hr Mn	Dy Hr Mn	Dy Hr Mn	1 OCTOBER 1967
☽0S 3 12:13	♀ ♍ 1 18:07	1 3:14 ♀ ☌	♍ 1 3:38	31 2:47 ♄ ☍	♏ 1 15:26	3 20:24 ● 9♎56	Julian Day # 24745
☽0N 16 18:38	♃ ♍ 19 10:51	2 21:43 ♅ ☌	♎ 3 4:34	3 10:55 ♅ ⚹	♐ 3 14:51	10 12:11 ☽ 16♑30	Delta T 38.1 sec
♄⚼♆ 16 18:07	♂ ♑ 23 2:14	5 0:13 ♃ ⚹	♏ 5 4:14	5 11:47 ♅ □	♑ 5 15:44	18 10:11 ○ 24♈21	SVP 05♓42'45"
☿ R 21 5:15	☉ ♏ 24 2:44	7 1:00 ♃ □	♐ 7 4:32	7 16:09 ♀ △	♒ 7 19:45	18 10:15 •T 1.143	Obliquity 23°26'45"
☽0S 30 23:19		9 3:59 ♃ △	♑ 9 7:04	9 15:50 ♆ □	♓ 10 3:42	26 12:04 ☾ 2♌23	⚷ Chiron 27♓05.1R
	♀ ♎ 9 16:32	11 5:50 ♅ △	♒ 11 12:45	12 10:52 ♅ ☍	♈ 12 14:58		☽ Mean ☊ 28♈51.8
☿ D 10 16:16	☉ ♐ 23 0:04	13 19:47 ♃ ☍	♓ 13 21:38	14 0:05 ♂ □	♉ 15 3:52	2 5:48 ● 9♏07	
♀0S 12 3:36		16 1:59 ♅ ☍	♈ 16 8:58	17 13:00 ♅ △	♊ 17 16:40	2 5:38:17 •T non-C	1 NOVEMBER 1967
☽0N 13 0:37		18 21:30 ♃ △	♉ 18 21:41	20 0:51 ♅ □	♋ 20 4:13	9 1:00 ☽ 15♒56	Julian Day # 24776
♄0S 18 9:03		21 4:12 ♅ △	♊ 21 10:38	22 12:54 ☉ △	♌ 22 13:47	17 4:53 ○ 24♉09	Delta T 38.1 sec
☽0S 27 8:37		23 22:04 ☉ △	♋ 23 22:27	24 10:38 ♆ □	♍ 24 20:46	25 0:23 ☾ 2♍02	SVP 05♓42'42"
		26 2:16 ♅ ⚹	♌ 26 7:40	26 22:20 ♅ ☌	♎ 27 0:48		Obliquity 23°26'45"
		28 1:44 ♆ □	♍ 28 13:19	28 22:37 ♂ □	♏ 29 2:13		⚷ Chiron 25♓52.6R
		30 11:09 ♅ ☌	♎ 30 15:31				☽ Mean ☊ 27♈13.3

Figure Copyright © 1994, Neil F. Michelsen [Callouts Added]

That's the bad news. The good news is that because Chiron moves so slowly, we can still get a reasonably accurate position for Chiron with only a few modifications to our basic process. Once again, here's the table with the start and end positions of Chiron for my birth chart filled in.

Planet Travel (PT) (UT÷24 hrs)   0.116

Planet	Start	End	Total Travel	Travel x PT	Birth Position
☉	0♏52'58"	1♏52'47"	59.8167'	6'56"	1♏00'
☽	13♋11'18"	25♋52'33"	12.6875°	1°28'18"	14♋39
☿	16♏20.7℞	15♏43.7℞	37'	4.292'	16♏16 ℞
⚷	27♓05.0℞	25♓52.6℞			

In my case, Chiron is retrograde, so we'll subtract the end position from the start position to find its total travel distance. If Chiron were direct, you would, of course, subtract the start position from the end position.

$$\begin{array}{rcccl} 27♓05.0 & = & 27°05.0 & = & 26°65.0 \\ -25♓52.6 & = & 25°52.6 & = & 25°52.6 \\ \hline \end{array}$$

1°12.4 = 1°12 = 72 minutes Total Travel.

Planet Travel (PT) (UT÷24 hrs)   0.116

Planet	Start	End	Total Travel	Travel x PT	Birth Position
☉	0♏52'58"	1♏52'47"	59.8167'	6'56"	1♏00'
☽	13♋11'18"	25♋52'33"	12.6875	1°28'18"	14♋39
☿	16♏20.7℞	15♏43.7℞	37'	4.292'	16♏16 ℞
⚷	27♓05.0℞	25♓52.6℞	**72'**		

Here's where we have to make some adjustments. We can't use the **PT** constant that we've been using, because that relates to travel over a 24-hour period, and the total travel we have for Chiron is the distance traveled over the ***entire calendar month.*** Since Chiron moves so slowly, we're simply going to figure out approximately where Chiron would be on the ***date of birth*** and not worry about the daily motion.

To do this, we need to create a new constant, using the same principles. Take the ***date of birth*** and divide it by the ***total number of days in the month of birth.*** In my case, the UT date of my birth is the 25th of October. Since October has 31 days, we divide 25 by 31 and come up with 0.8064. **This is the PT constant we will use for Chiron only** to find the approximate ΔP.

72 minutes travel x 0.8064 **PT** = 58.06 minutes ΔP.

We then add this result to the table in the Travel x **PT** column.

NOTE: It's essential that you divide the date by the correct number of days in the month! If the **UT** of birth was 25 February 1967, you would divide 25 by 28 days and get 0.8929 as your Chiron **PT** constant.

Lesson 4: Interpolating the Planets

Planet Travel (PT) (UT÷24 hrs)   0.116

Planet	Start	End	Total Travel	Travel x PT	Birth Position
☉	0♏52'58"	1♏52'47"	59.8167'	6'56"	1♏00'
☽	13♋11'18"	25♋52'33"	12.6875	1°28'18"	14♋39
☿	16♏20.7℞	15♏43.7℞	37'	4.292'	16♏16 ℞
⚷	27♓05.0℞	25♓52.6℞	72'	**58.06'**	

Since Chiron is retrograde in my chart, we subtract the ΔP from the start position to find the approximate position of Chiron in my chart.

$$27♓05.0 = 26°65.0$$
$$- 58.06 = 58.06$$
$$26°06.94 = 26♓07 \text{ Chiron}$$

Planet Travel (PT) (UT÷24 hrs)   0.116

Planet	Start	End	Total Travel	Travel x PT	Birth Position
☉	0♏52'58"	1♏52'47"	59.8167'	6'56"	1♏00'
☽	13♋11'18"	25♋52'33"	12.6875	1°28'18"	14♋39
☿	16♏20.7℞	15♏43.7℞	37'	4.292'	16♏16 ℞
⚷	27♓05.0℞	25♓52.6℞	72'	58.06'	**26♓07 ℞**

Exercises Part 2: Calculate the PT and Interpolate the Birth Positions of the Following:

6.

Universal Time (UT) of Birth   August 6, 1972 15:28

Planet Travel (PT) (UT÷24 hrs)

Planet	Start	End	Total Travel	Travel x PT	Birth Position
☉	13♌37'23"	14♌34'54"			

7.

Universal Time (UT) of Birth   March 14, 1966 21:15

Planet Travel (PT) (UT÷24 hrs)

Planet	Start	End	Total Travel	Travel x PT	Birth Position
☽	22♐48'15"	5♑09'04"			

8.

Universal Time (UT) of Birth   February 5, 1966 10:48

Planet Travel (PT) (UT÷24 hrs)

Planet	Start	End	Total Travel	Travel x PT	Birth Position
♃	27♌59.8℞	27♌52.2℞			

9.

Universal Time (UT) of Birth: May 6, 1961

Planet Travel (PT) (day of month ÷ total days in month)

Planet	Start	End	Total Travel	Travel x PT	Birth Position
⚷	5♓56.5	6♓39.4			

10.

Universal Time (UT) of Birth: July 19, 1972 04:55

Planet Travel (PT) (UT÷24 hrs)

Planet	Start	End	Total Travel	Travel x PT	Birth Position
☽	3♏50'45"	15♏43'51"			

11.

Universal Time (UT) of Birth: April 14, 1974 12:37

Planet Travel (PT) (UT÷24 hrs)

Planet	Start	End	Total Travel	Travel x PT	Birth Position
☉	23♈40'12"	24♈38'58"			

12.

Universal Time (UT) of Birth: January 26, 1978 21:12

Planet Travel (PT) (UT÷24 hrs)

Planet	Start	End	Total Travel	Travel x PT	Birth Position
♂	0♌1.9℞	29♋38.6℞			

Lesson 5: Finding the Sidereal Time of Birth

In addition to the Birth Time (Local Time), and **Universal Time of Birth**, there is one more time calculation that we will need in order to be able to calculate the house cusp positions in the chart: the **Sidereal Time of Birth.** Sidereal time is the "star time" based on the fixed stars. Sidereal time is calculated based on the period of time that it takes the Earth to return to a point where the same fixed star is visible at the same angle and the same relative position. A **Sidereal Day** is actually about 4 minutes shorter than a **Solar Day.**

In order to calculate the **Sidereal Time of Birth,** we need some information from the **Atlas** and from the **Ephemeris**. In addition to the **Universal Time of Birth** (which we learned how to calculate back in Lesson 2), we need the following information:

1. **Longitude Time Equivalent** from the **Atlas** for the Location of Birth
2. **Solar Sidereal Correction** from the **Atlas**
3. **Sidereal Time** listed in the **Ephemeris** for Midnight or Noon **Universal Time** (depending on which Ephemeris you use) on the date of Birth. We'll be using a **Midnight Ephemeris** by Neil F. Michelsen, published by Astro Communications Services.

Let's take a moment and really look at how to use *The American Atlas* to look up time zone and location information. Taking, for example, New Orleans, Louisiana, where I was born, the entry in the Atlas looks something like this:

New Orleans   36   2   29N57'16   90W47'01   6:00:18

Even though this doesn't look particularly helpful at first glance, it really does contain a great deal of essential information. First of all, it contains the **Latitude** and **Longitude** coordinates for New Orleans (29 degrees 57 minutes 16 seconds North, 90 degrees 47 minutes 1 second West) and it's a good idea to jot these down for future reference—we're going to need them later. The last number in the row, the "6:00:18" is the **Longitude Time Equivalent.** This is very important, so write it down—we need this to calculate the **Sidereal Time.**

The "36" that follows "New Orleans" is the County Code, which is a cross-reference to a table found before each State listing that shows all of the counties (or in the case of Louisiana, Parishes) in the state. This is helpful, particularly when a state has more than one city with the same name.

The "2," however, is very important. This column refers to the **Time Table** in effect for the city in question. Also at the beginning of each State listing in the Atlas, one or more Time Tables appear, detailing the time changes (and time-zone offsets) for each location. The "2" means we would look at "LA#2" in the Time Table listing.

The last date listed is 4/30/1967 at 02:00 (which, since my date of birth is 10/24/67, applies to this example), and it refers us to "US#1" for the Standard U.S. Daylight Table. This means that as of April 30, 1967, Louisiana standardized its time changes to those of the rest of the country. It also means we have to go to another table to find out if Standard Time or Daylight Savings Time was in effect. Before we go to that table, however, make note that the earlier listings all start with a "C" which means that we will be dealing with the Central Time Zone. We turn to the US#1 Table, and look up the date of birth, 10/24/67. We see that on 1/30/67 DT (Daylight Time) went into effect, and on 10/29/67, the time changed back to ST (Standard Time). So on 10/24/67, the time zone in effect was CDT for Central Daylight Time.

Looking up CDT in the Time Zones and Abbreviations table, we see that the time zone offset to Greenwich Mean Time is 5:00. Since Louisiana is **west of Greenwich,** we would **add** this number to the local time of birth to find the Universal Time of Birth.

The last figure we need to look up is the **Solar-Sidereal Time Correction,** which we can find in the **Solar-Sidereal Time Correction (Acceleration)** table in the Atlas. To use this table, we start with the minutes of the UT of birth, and locate the row with that number. Then we look across the table to find the column with the corresponding hours of the UT of birth. The number we find there (expressed in minutes and seconds) is the **Solar-Sidereal Time Correction.** Make note of this number.

In my case, the **Universal Time** of my birth is 02:47 on October 25, 1967, and the **Solar-Sidereal Time Correction** is 0:27 (27 seconds).

Some Definitions and Explanations Before We Proceed

The **Solar-Sidereal Correction** is needed to compensate for the difference between the **Sidereal Day** and the standard **Mean Solar Day** (i.e., clock time). The **Sidereal Day** is actually only 23 hours 56 minutes and 3 seconds long, in terms of clock time. While the Ephemeris lists the correct **Sidereal Time** for each date at Midnight, by the end of the day, the clock time and the **Sidereal Time** have once again come out of sync to the tune of 3 minutes and 57 seconds by the end of the day. Since the stars don't care what time we think it is here on Earth, we need to compensate for the daily difference between the **Universal Time of Birth** and the actual **Sidereal Time of Birth** by adding the appropriate **Solar-Sidereal Correction**.

The **Longitude Time Equivalent** is needed to compensate for the longitude of the birth place. The creation of Time Zones helps to standardize everyone on the same local time, and the zones are set at 15° intervals of Longitude starting at Greenwich, England, with each zone representing (usually) a 1-hour increment from the previous one. Clock time, however, is very different from **Sidereal Time** (star time), and even though, for example, Maine and Michigan are both in the Eastern Time Zone and share the same clock time, the Sun and the Fixed Stars do not rise at the same time in Maine as they do in Michigan, because of the difference in longitude. At the same moment in time, Michigan may still have sunlight, but the Sun will have already set in Maine—even though in both states, the clock time is the same.

What we're looking for when we calculate the **Sidereal Time** is an idea of exactly where the Earth was in its rotation with respect to the fixed stars at the time of birth—and again, the stars don't care what time we think it is. Every 1° of longitude means a change of approximately 4 minutes in time. We use the **Longitude Time Equivalent** to make the appropriate adjustments.

Calculating the Sidereal Time of Birth

Once we've made note of the necessary information, calculating the **Sidereal Time of Birth** is very simple:

```
    Universal Time of Birth
  + Solar-Sidereal Correction (SSC)
  + Midnight Sidereal Time from Ephemeris
  − Longitude Time Equivalent
    ─────────────────────────────────────
    Sidereal Time of Birth
```

Let's take my birth information once again as the example: October 24, 1967 9:47 P.M. CDT, New Orleans, LA. Here are the appropriate constants and conversions:

UT of Birth:	October 25, 1967 02:47:00
Solar-Sidereal Correction (SSC):	00:00:27 *(Minutes and Seconds, remember?)*
Midnight Sidereal Time:	02:10:47 *(October 25, 1967—the UT Date of Birth)*
Longitude Time Equivalent:	06:00:18 *(From the American Atlas)*

And the calculations go something like this:

	UT of Birth:	02:47:00		
+	Midnight Sidereal Time:	02:10:47		
		04:57:47		
+	Solar-Sidereal Correction (SSC):	00:00:27		
		04:57:74	=	28:57:74
−	Longitude Time Equivalent	06:00:18	=	06:00:18
	SIDEREAL TIME OF BIRTH			22:57:56

Some of you may be wondering just what happened in those last few lines—specifically, how we got from 04:57:74 to 28:57:74. The answer is simple: not only don't the stars care what time it is on the clock, but *they also don't care what day it is on the calendar.* If the **Longitude Time Equivalent** is larger than the number from which it is being subtracted, simply add a day (24 hours) to the first number and then subtract. By the same token, if the answer for the **Sidereal Time of Birth** turns out to be more than 24 hours, simply subtract the extra 24 hours to get the final result. **Sidereal time is always expressed within the range of 0 to 24 hours.**

Here's another example of calculating the **Sidereal Time of Birth:**

UT of Birth:	May 11, 1931 17:30:00, New York, NY
Solar-Sidereal Correction (SSC):	00:02:52
Midnight Sidereal Time:	15:11:16
Longitude Time Equivalent:	04:55:48

And the calculations go something like this:

	UT of Birth:	17:30:00
+	Midnight Sidereal Time:	15:11:16
		32:41:16
+	Solar-Sidereal Correction (SSC):	00:02:52
		32:43:68
−	Longitude Time Equivalent	04:55:48
		27:48:20
−	24 Hours to Adjust Range	24:00:00
	SIDEREAL TIME OF BIRTH	3:48:20

Notice that we don't bother to make proper adjustments to the time until we get the final result. In the above example, one of the interim answers is 32:43:68 and even though we can fudge the sidereal hours by adding or subtracting 24, we can't fudge the seconds and technically need to change this to 32:44:08. Since we will be adding and subtracting more to this number, however, we can skip this step. We do have to remember, however, to make the proper changes to the final answer so that it is expressed in the correct time format.

Sidereal Time in Eastern and Southern Hemisphere Charts

Calculating the **Sidereal Time** for charts in the Eastern Hemisphere is exactly the same as for charts in the Western Hemisphere. The only difference is that we end up *adding* the **Longitude Time Equivalent** instead of subtracting it. This isn't quite as obvious as it might seem, and to make things even more confusing, the **Longitude Time Equivalents** in the *International Atlas* for the Eastern Hemisphere are represented as *negative* numbers. For those of you who have this information buried in repressed traumatic memories of math class, *subtracting a negative number* is the same thing as *adding a positive number.* Rather than dealing with the (literal) double negative, simply ignore the negative sign and add the **Longitude Time Equivalent** when calculating an Eastern Hemisphere **Sidereal Time.**

Calculating the **Sidereal Time** for charts in the Southern Hemisphere is exactly the same as for charts in the Northern Hemisphere. The only difference is that if you are using a **Table of Houses** calculated for the *Northern Hemisphere* to calculate a chart for the *Southern Hemisphere*, the **very last step is to add 12 hours to the result,** and then adjust it again so that it fits within the 0 to 24 hour range. Since we will be working with a **Table of Houses** for the Northern Hemisphere (and you'll be presumably using a Northern Hemisphere Table of Houses when you take the exams), when calculating the **Sidereal Time** for a Southern Hemisphere chart, we will calculate the "fudged" time.

The following example takes both Eastern Hemisphere and Southern Hemisphere adjustments into account: a chart for Perth, Australia.

UT of Birth:	September 8, 1972 18:36 [Perth, Australia]
Solar-Sidereal Correction (SSC):	00:03:03
Midnight Sidereal Time:	23:08:37
Longitude Time Equivalent:	– 07:43:20

And the calculations go something like this:

	UT of Birth:	18:36:00	
+	Midnight Sidereal Time:	23:08:37	
		41:44:37	
+	Solar-Sidereal Correction (SSC):	00:03:03	
		41:47:40	
+	Longitude Time Equivalent	07:43:20	←ADD for EASTERN
		48:90:60	
+	12 Hours For Southern Hemisphere	12:00:00	← Adjust for SOUTHERN
		60:90:60 = 61:31:00	
−	24 Hours to Adjust Range	24:00:00	
		37:31:00	
−	24 Hours to Adjust Range (Again)	24:00:00	
	SIDEREAL TIME OF BIRTH	13:31:00	

This particular example required a lot of adjustments! First of all, notice that we converted the minutes and seconds into acceptable units and 60:90:60 became 61:31:00. Since this is obviously not within the 0 to 24 hour range of acceptable sidereal times, we subtract 24 hours—not once, but *twice*—until we come up with a time that is within the acceptable range.

Exercises: Calculate the Sidereal Time

1. UT of Birth: June 22, 1954 04:29, Chicago, IL   Midnight Sidereal Time: 17:58:34
   SSC: 00:44   Longitude Time Equivalent: 05:50:36

2. UT of Birth: May 31, 1969 17:14, Honolulu, HI   Midnight Sidereal Time: 16:33:16
   SSC: 02:50   Longitude Time Equivalent: 10:31:26

3. UT of Birth: Nov. 4, 1958, 10:15 New York, NY   Midnight Sidereal Time: 02:50:56
   SSC: 01:41   Longitude Time Equivalent: 04:56:02

4. UT of Birth: March 5, 1970, 22:45, New Orleans, LA   Midnight Sidereal Time: 10:49:18
   SSC: 03:44   Longitude Time Equivalent: 06:00:18

5. UT of Birth: Jan 4, 1948, 06:40, San Diego, CA   Midnight Sidereal Time: 06:50:05
   SSC: 01:06   Longitude Time Equivalent: 07:48:38

6. UT of Birth: April 19, 1975, 16:25, London, England   Midnight Sidereal Time: 13:45:54
   SSC: 02:42   Longitude Time Equivalent: 00:00:40

7. UT of Birth: July 8, 1961, 20:09, Manaus, Brazil   Midnight Sidereal Time: 19:02:49
   SSC: 03:19   Longitude Time Equivalent: 04:00:04
   NOTE: Southern Hemisphere Chart

8. UT of Birth: Dec. 13, 1948, 12:45, Hamburg, Germany   Midnight Sidereal Time: 05:26:20
   SSC: 02:06   Longitude Time Equivalent: −00:39:56
   NOTE: Eastern Hemisphere Chart

9. UT of Birth: May 15, 1982, 02:22, Karos, South Africa   Midnight Sidereal Time: 15:29:35
   SSC: 00:23   Longitude Time Equivalent: −01:26:20
   NOTE: Southern and Eastern Hemisphere

10. UT of Birth: May 1, 1967, 23:43, Darwin, Australia Midnight Sidereal Time: 14:32:56
    SSC: 03:54 Longitude Time Equivalent: −08:43:20
    NOTE: Southern and Eastern Hemisphere

Lesson 6: Interpolating the Angles and House Cusps

The last thing that we need to do to calculate a natal chart is to locate the house cusps and angles. In order to do this, we will need the **Sidereal Time of Birth** (which we just calculated), the **Latitude and Longitude of the birth location** (which we found in the Atlas), and a **book of tables** for the house system we plan to use. We will also have to calculate two more constants, the **Sidereal Differential (SD)** and the **Latitude Differential (LD).** Below is an example of the **Koch** tables we will need to calculate the house cusps in my natal chart. Again, please do purchase your own copy of the *Michelsen Book of Tables* from ACS Publications at 1-800-514-5070.

Figure Copyright ©1985, Neil F. Michelsen. Callouts Added

In these examples, we will be working with the **Koch house system,** because I personally use Koch houses for my natal charts.

Notice how the tables are incremented based on 1° of Right Ascension (R.A.), which is equivalent to 4 minutes of **Sidereal Time.** Each table includes the longitude of the Midheaven for the Right Ascension/Sidereal Time, and then a list of the positions for the Ascendant, and the cusps of the 11th, 12th, 2nd and 3rd houses for different Latitudes, from 0° to 60° North. We only need to calculate the positions of these six cusps, because the remaining house cusps will, of course, have the exact same degrees, in the opposite signs.

Unlike the planets, when we interpolate the house cusps and angles, we will be interpolating *twice*: the first time will be **across two tables to find the Longitudinal positions;** the second time will be **down one table to compensate for the differences in Latitude.** The only exception is when we interpolate the Midheaven, which is the same regardless of the Latitude. Below is a diagram that shows what we're going to be doing when we interpolate the house cusps. Please don't panic! We will break things down into small, easy-to-understand steps. I promise.

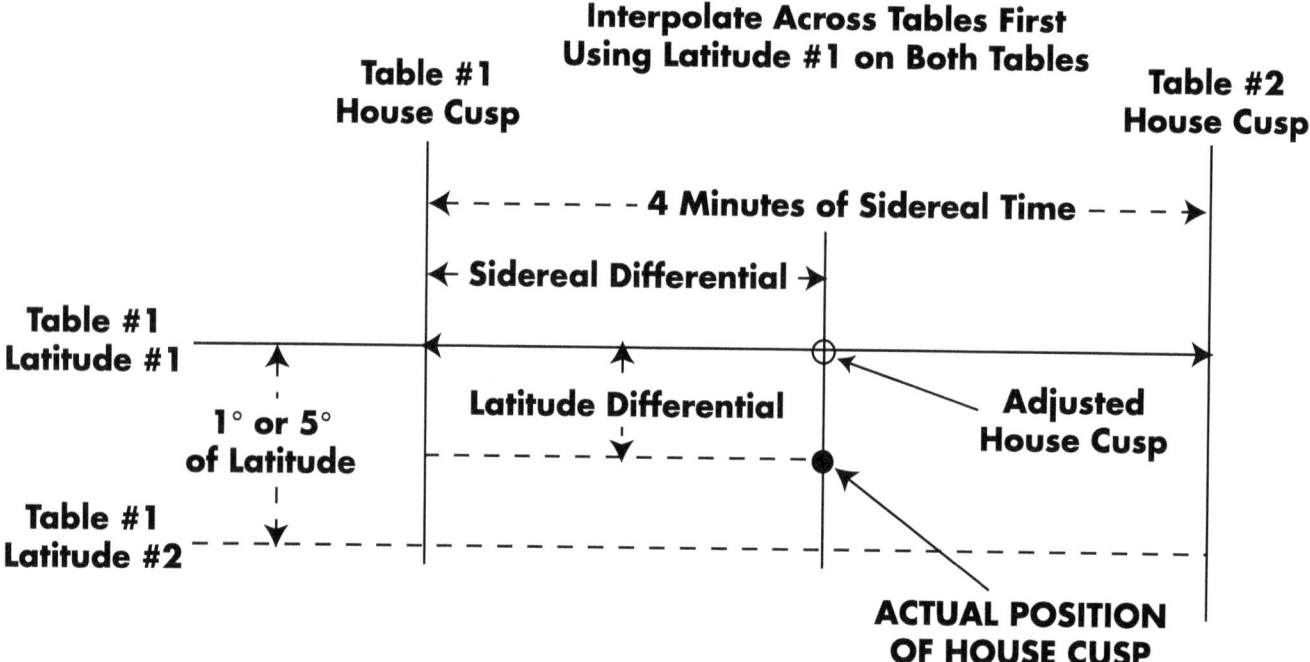

Finding the Sidereal Differential (SD)

The first thing we will do is calculate the two constants we will need to interpolate the cusps. The first constant is called the **Sidereal Differential (SD),** and it will be used to **interpolate between the positions listed for two sidereal times.** In order to do this, we have to figure out exactly which tables we need, and we do this by looking up the two tables that are the closest to the **Sidereal Time of Birth.**

Using my **Sidereal Time of Birth**, which, you recall from the previous lesson, is 22:57:56, we find that the two closest tables are the ones for 22h 56m 0s and for 23h 00m 0s. We need to find out where my **Sidereal Time** falls between these two sidereal times, just as when we interpolated the planets, we needed to find out where the **Universal Time of Birth** fell in the 24-hour day.

With the **Sidereal Differential**, we're not looking at 24 hours; instead, we're looking at only **4 minutes of sidereal time.** Here is how we calculate the **Sidereal Differential**.

❶ Subtract the Smaller **Sidereal Time** from the **Sidereal Time of Birth**
❷ Convert the result (which will be between 0 and 4 minutes) in terms of minutes by dividing by 60 seconds.
❸ Express the difference in terms of minutes.
❹ Divide the result by 4 minutes to find the **Sidereal Differential**.

Using my **Sidereal Time of Birth,** here's how this would look:

a.	Sidereal Time of Birth	22:57:56
	– Smaller Sidereal Time from Table	22:56:00
		00:01:56
b.	Divide Seconds by 60 for Minutes:	01 minute + [56 seconds ÷ 60 = 0.9333]
c.	Difference in Terms of Minutes:	1.9333 minutes
d.	Divide by 4 minutes for SD:	1.9333 minutes ÷ 4 minutes = **0.4833 SD**

Once you calculate the **Sidereal Differential,** write it down in the designated space(s) on the **Natal Chart Calculation Worksheet.** You will refer to it every time you interpolate between the two tables.

Finding the Latitude Differential (LD)

We find the **Latitude Differential (LD)** in the same way as we do the **Sidereal Differential.** The only difference is that the latitudes are listed in different increments: from 0° to 20°, latitude is listed in 5° increments; from 21° to 60°, latitude is listed in 1° increments. This is important to note, because it will change how we find the **LD**.

We use the **latitude of birth** to determine the two latitude coordinates we will use for the interpolation. New Orleans, where I was born, is at 29N57′16″ latitude (from the **Atlas**). This falls neatly between 29°N and 30°N, so these are the two coordinates we will be using. We follow the same process here as with the **Sidereal Differential:**

❶ Subtract the Smaller Latitude from Latitude of Birth
❷ Convert the result in terms of degrees.
❸ Divide the result by the difference between the two listings in the table: 1° if greater than 20° latitude, 5° if between 0° and 20° latitude.

In my case it looks something like this:

a. Latitude of Birth   29N57'16"
   − Smaller Latitude from Table   29N00'00"
                                              57'16"

b. Divide Seconds by 60 for Minutes: 57 min + [16 seconds ÷ 60 = .2667 min]

c. Difference in Terms of Minutes: 57.2667 minutes

d. Convert to Degrees: 57.2667 min ÷ 60 = 0.9544 degrees

e. Divide by Table Difference for LD: 0.9544° ÷ 1° = **0.9544 LD**

Once you calculate the **Latitude Differential,** write it down in the designated space(s) on the **Natal Chart Calculation Worksheet.** You will refer to it every time you interpolate the latitude.

Exercises Part 1: Find the SD and LD

	Sidereal Time of Birth	Sidereal Time Table #1	Sidereal Time Table #1	SD
1.	22:16:49	22 h 16 m 0 s	22 h 20 m 0 s	
2.	01:09:22	1h 8m 0s	1h 12m 0s	
3.	04:54:20	4h 52m 0s	4h 56m 0s	
4.	14:18:59	14h 16m 0s	14h 20m 0s	

	Latitude of Birth	Latitude #1	Latitude #2	LD
5.	34N21'12"	34N	35N	
6.	42N46'59"	42N	43N	
7.	13N37'42"	10N	15N	
8.	9N04'20"	5N	10N	

Interpolating the Midheaven

We'll start by interpolating the Midheaven. **Since the Midheaven is the same regardless of the latitude, we only have to interpolate once, between the two tables.** The process is exactly the same as when we interpolate the positions of the planets. Using my chart, we get the following:

SD = 0.4833

Table 1 MC	Table 2 MC	Difference	Difference x SD	Natal MC
12♓39	13♓43			

The first thing that we must do, of course, is determine the difference between the two Midheaven positions. We will then convert this number into minutes, and multiply it by the SD. Since the Midheaven is advancing in direct motion, we'll then add this result to the earlier Midheaven position to find the Midheaven for the chart.

```
  Table 2 Midheaven Position      13♓43
– Table 1 Midheaven Position      12♓39
                                  01° 04' = [1 x 60] min. + 4 min. = 64 minutes
```

SD = 0.4833

Table 1 MC	Table 2 MC	Difference	Difference x SD	Natal MC
12♓39	13♓43	**64'**		

We multiply this result by the SD to find the travel distance, and enter it in the table.

64 minutes x 0.4833 = 30.9312 minutes.

SD = 0.4833

Table 1 MC	Table 2 MC	Difference	Difference x SD	Natal MC
12♓39	13♓43	64'	**31'**	

Notice that we have rounded the result to the nearest whole minute. When calculating the house cusps, we don't need to worry about seconds of arc.

The last step is to add this difference to the Table 1 Midheaven position to find the Natal MC, and note it in the table.

```
  Table 1 Midheaven Position      12♓39
+ [Difference x SD]               00° 31
                                  12♓70 = 13♓10 Midheaven
```

SD = 0.4833

Table 1 MC	Table 2 MC	Difference	Difference x SD	Natal MC
12♓39	13♓43	64'	31'	**13♓10**

Interpolating the Remaining House Cusps

To interpolate the remaining five cusps, we will need to interpolate twice: first **across the two tables** as we did with the Midheaven, and then make an adjustment by interpolating **down the first table between the two Latitude Coordinates.** When we interpolate across the tables, we'll always use the row that corresponds to the smaller latitude. Taking my chart as an example, the two Latitudes we use to calculate the LD are 29°N and 30°N. When we interpolate between the two tables, we read the positions from the 29°N rows. We'll start by calculating the Ascendant of my chart.

SD = 0.4833

Cusp	Table 1	Table 2	Difference	Difference x SD	Adjusted Cusp
Ascendant	28♊04	29♊00			

The first thing that we must do is determine the difference between the two cusp positions by subtracting the value in Table 1 from the value in Table 2. We will then convert this number into minutes.

$$\begin{array}{r} \text{Table 2 Ascendant Position} \quad 29♊00 \\ - \text{ Table 1 Ascendant Position} \quad 28♊04 \\ \hline 56' \end{array}$$

Since the result is already expressed in terms of minutes, we don't need to convert it.

SD = 0.4833

Cusp	Table 1	Table 2	Difference	Difference x SD	Adjusted Cusp
Ascendant	28♊04	29♊00	56'		

We'll multiply the difference by the SD and record the result in the table, rounded to the nearest whole minute.

56 minutes x 0.4833 = 27.0648 minutes = 27 minutes.

SD = 0.4833

Cusp	Table 1	Table 2	Difference	Difference x SD	Adjusted Cusp
Ascendant	28♊04	29♊00	56'	27'	

And since the coordinates in Table 2 are greater than those in Table 1, we'll add this amount to the Table 1 position to find the **Adjusted Ascendant.**

Table 1 Ascendant Position   28♊04
+ [Difference x SD]   00° 27
———————————————
28♊31 Adjusted Ascendant

SD = 0.4833

Cusp	Table 1	Table 2	Difference	Difference x SD	Adjusted Cusp
Ascendant	28♊04	29♊00	56'	27'	28♊31

Next, we move to the Latitude table where we will calculate the final house cusp positions. In this table, we will use the cusp positions **from Table 1 only**, at both of the latitude coordinates (in this example, at 29° N and at 30° N).

LD = 0.9544

Cusp	Table 1 Latitude 1	Table 1 Latitude 2	Difference	Difference x LD	Adjusted Cusp (Copy from Above)	ACTUAL HOUSE CUSP
ASC	28♊04	28♊37			28♊31	

Look familiar? It should. We're going to interpolate between the Table 1 Latitude and Table 2 Latitude, in exactly the same way as we did between the two tables. The only difference is that sometimes when increasing in Latitude, the cusp positions actually move backward (similar to a planet in retrograde motion). **If the Table 1 position is greater than the Table 2 position, make special note of it, and simply subtract the Table 2 position from the Table 1 position.** In my case, the cusps are increasing with Latitude, so we'll subtract the Table 1 value from the Table 2 value.

Table 1 Latitude Position 2   28♊37
− Table 1 Latitude Position 1   28♊04
———————————————
33'

Again, the result is already expressed in minutes, so we don't need to convert it; we can simply make note of it in the table.

LD = 0.9544

Cusp	Table 1 Latitude 1	Table 1 Latitude 2	Difference	Difference x LD	Adjusted Cusp (Copy from Above)	ACTUAL HOUSE CUSP
ASC	28♊04	28♊37	33'		28♊31	

And as with all of the other interpolations, we multiply the difference by the **LD**, round it to the nearest whole minute, and enter the result in the next space in the table like so:

33 minutes x 0.9544 **LD** = 31.4952 minutes

LD = 0.9544

Cusp	Table 1 Latitude 1	Table 1 Latitude 2	Difference	Difference x LD	Adjusted Cusp (Copy from Above)	ACTUAL HOUSE CUSP
ASC	28♊04	28♊37	33'	31'	28♊31	

IMPORTANT: This is Where Things Change!!

The last step is the only one that is a bit different. We will either add or subtract the result from the **Adjusted Cusp Position**—*not* from the Table 1 position. If Latitude 2's position is *greater than* Latitude 1's position, we will **add** to the **Adjusted Cusp** to find the **Actual House Cusp**. If, on the other hand, Latitude 2's position is *less than* Latitude 1's position (if the cusp is moving backwards), we will **subtract** this number from the **Adjusted Cusp** to find the **Actual House Cusp**. This can change from cusp to cusp, so you must always check before you perform this final step!

In my case, since the Latitude 2 position is greater than the Latitude 1 position, we will **add** the difference to the **Adjusted House Cusp** to find the **Actual House Cusp**.

```
Adjusted Ascendant Position:       28♊31
+ [Difference x [LD]               00° 31
                                   ─────────
                                   28♊62  = 29♊02 Ascendant
```

LD = 0.9544

Cusp	Table 1 Latitude 1	Table 1 Latitude 2	Difference	Difference x LD	Adjusted Cusp (Copy from Above)	ACTUAL HOUSE CUSP
ASC	28♊04	28♊37	33'	31'	28♊31	29♊02

Exercises Part 2: Calculate the Remaining House Cusps

9. Now it's your turn. See if you can calculate the rest of the house cusps for my chart. I've filled in the information you will need, but make sure that you can look at the illustration of the tables at the beginning of this chapter, and see where the figures came from.

SD = 0.4833

Cusp	Table 1	Table 2	Difference	Difference x SD	Adjusted Cusp
Ascendant	28♊04	29♊00	56'	27'	28♊31
2nd	23♋26	24♋21			
3rd	17♌51	18♌51			
11th	23♈21	24♈31			
12th	29♉06	00♊07			

LD = 0.9544

Cusp	Table 1 Latitude 1	Table 1 Latitude 2	Difference	Difference x LD	Adjusted Cusp (Copy from Above)	ACTUAL HOUSE CUSP
ASC	28♊04	28♊37	33'	31'	28♊31	29♊02
2nd	23♋26	23♋50				
3rd	17♌51	18♌05				
11th	23♈21	23♈48				
12th	29♉06	29♉42				

Interpolating the Cusps for Charts in Other Hemispheres

By the time that we get to this point, we've already made most of the adjustments for hemispheres other than the North and West. The Eastern Hemisphere charts required adjustments in how we calculated the **Universal Time of Birth** and the **Sidereal Time of Birth**. And the Southern Hemisphere Charts, remember, had 12 hours added to the **Sidereal Time** to compensate for being below the equator. The last adjustment we have to make for a Southern Hemisphere chart is that once we've calculated the positions of the house cusps (using, of course, the correctly-fudged **Sidereal Time** for the Southern Hemisphere), we then use the opposite signs for the final cusps.

IMPORTANT NOTE: Remember that this applies only if you are calculating charts for the Southern Hemisphere and you are using a Northern Hemisphere table of houses. If you are using a Southern Hemisphere table of houses, you don't make any adjustments to anything for charts in the Southern Hemisphere; however, to calculate the angles in the Northern Hemisphere, you would need to subtract 12 hours from the Sidereal time and use the opposite signs for the final cusps.

IMPORTANT NOTE PART II: If you are checking your work using a computer to calculate the charts, *do not make any changes to the computer chart!* Computer chart calculation programs will automatically make the necessary adjustments when calculating charts in the Southern Hemisphere.

Exercises Part 3: Calculate the House Cusps for a Southern Hemisphere Chart

10. Here's another example of calculating house cusps (as well as a review of finding the SD and the LD). This time, the chart is for a location in Lima, Peru, 12S03, 77W03.

Sidereal Time of Birth (Adjusted): 5:57:24
Two Sidereal Times from Tables (for SD): 5h 56m 0s   6h 00m 0s
Two Closest Latitudes from Table (for LD): 10°   15°

SD = 0.35

Cusp	Table 1	Table 2	Difference	Difference x SD	Adjusted Cusp
Ascendant	28♍59	00♎00			
2nd	00♏29	01♏28			
3rd	00♐22	01♐17			
11th	27♋48	28♋43			
12th	27♌33	28♌32			

LD = 0.41

Cusp	Table 1 Latitude 1	Table 1 Latitude 2	Difference	Difference x LD	Adjusted Cusp (Copy from Above)	ACTUAL HOUSE CUSP
ASC	28♍59	29♍01				
2nd	00♏29	00♏11				
3rd	00♐22	29♏59				
11th	27♋48	28♋12				
12th	27♌33	27♌55				

Exercises Part 4: Calculate and Draw Natal Charts

OK, here's your final exam on natal chart calculations! Using the **Natal Calculation Worksheet** as your guide, calculate and draw the natal charts for the following examples. I've looked up and provided all of the information that you will need for these examples, but I do urge you to become familiar with the **Ephemeris**, the **Atlas**, and the **Book of Tables** so that you know how to look things up for yourself. Good luck!

NOTE: When you calculate the SD for these charts, remember that all **Sidereal Times** in the tables are in 4-minute increments. Once you calculate the **Sidereal Time** for the chart you can easily deduce the two sidereal times from the tables. For example, a **Sidereal Time** of 4:53:19 would fall between 4h 52m 0s and 4h 56m 0s.

NOTE: Chiron positions are provided from a **Chiron Ephemeris** and are **daily** positions. **Interpolate with the same constant (PT) you use for the rest of the planets in the chart.**

11.

Part I: Fill In These Blanks (Look Up Information in Ephemeris and Atlas)

Name	Meryl Streep	Time Zone Correction	EDT (+4:00)
Date and Time of Birth	June 22, 1949 8:05 AM	Longitude Time Equivalent	4:57:29
Location of Birth	Summit, New Jersey, USA	Solar Sidereal Correction	1:59
Latitude & Longitude	40N44'29" 74W21'36"	Midnight Sidereal Time	17:59:23

Part II: Calculate the Constants You Will Need

Universal Time (UT) of Birth _____

Sidereal Time of Birth _____

Planet Travel (PT) (UT÷24 hrs) _____

Sidereal Differential _____

Latitude Differential _____

REMEMBER: Add 12 Hours to the Sidereal Time if Southern Hemisphere Chart!

Part III: Interpolate the Planets

Planet	Start	End	Total Travel	Travel x PT	Birth Position
☉	0♋14'12"	1♋11'27"			
☽	8♉16'19"	20♉29'25"			
☿	10♊2.7	10♊32.6			
♀	17♋48.3	19♋1.6			
♂	8♊28.7	9♊10.8			
♃	0♒34.7 ℞	0♒29.0 ℞			
♄	1♍31.7	1♍36.6			
♆	4♐14.7 ℞	4♐11.1 ℞			
♅	0♋42.3	0♋45.9			
♆	12♎23.8 ℞	12♎23.7			
♇	14♌50.4	14♌51.8			
☊	23♈29.5 ℞	23♈26.4 ℞			

REMEMBER: If the planet is in Retrograde motion, SUBTRACT the Travel x PT from the Start Position to get the Birth Position!

Part IV: Interpolate the House Cusps

(Copy the Constants you will need from Page 1)

Sidereal Time of Birth _____

Sidereal Differential (SD) _____

Latitude Differential (LD) _____

Part IV(a): Calculate the Midheaven

Table 1 MC	Table 2 MC	Difference	Difference x SD	Natal MC
18♈26	19♈30			

Part IV(b): Calculate the Ascendant and the other House Cusps starting with the ADJUSTED Positions

Cusp	Table 1	Table 2	Difference	Difference x SD	Adjusted Cusp
Ascendant	2♌12	2♌59			
2ⁿᵈ	27♌26	28♌19			
3ʳᵈ	22♍52	23♍51			
11ᵗʰ	3♊37	4♊30			
12ᵗʰ	5♋40	6♋27			

Part IV(c): Calculate the Final House Cusp Positions

Cusp	Table 1 Latitude 1	Table 1 Latitude 2	Difference	Difference x LD	Adjusted Cusp (Copy from Above)	ACTUAL HOUSE CUSP
ASC	2♌12	2♌42				
2ⁿᵈ	27♌26	27♌48				
3ʳᵈ	22♍52	23♍03				
11ᵗʰ	3♊37	4♊16				
12ᵗʰ	5♋40	6♋19				

REMEMBER: If the signs are moving forward as you increase in Latitude, you ADD the Difference x LD to the Adjusted Cusp to find the Actual House Cusp. If the signs are moving backwards, you SUBTRACT the Difference x LD from the Adjusted Cusp to find the Actual House Cusp.

SOUTHERN HEMISPHERE CHARTS: Use the OPPOSITE SIGN of the Actual House Cusps as your final answer.

Lesson 6: Interpolating the Angles and House Cusps

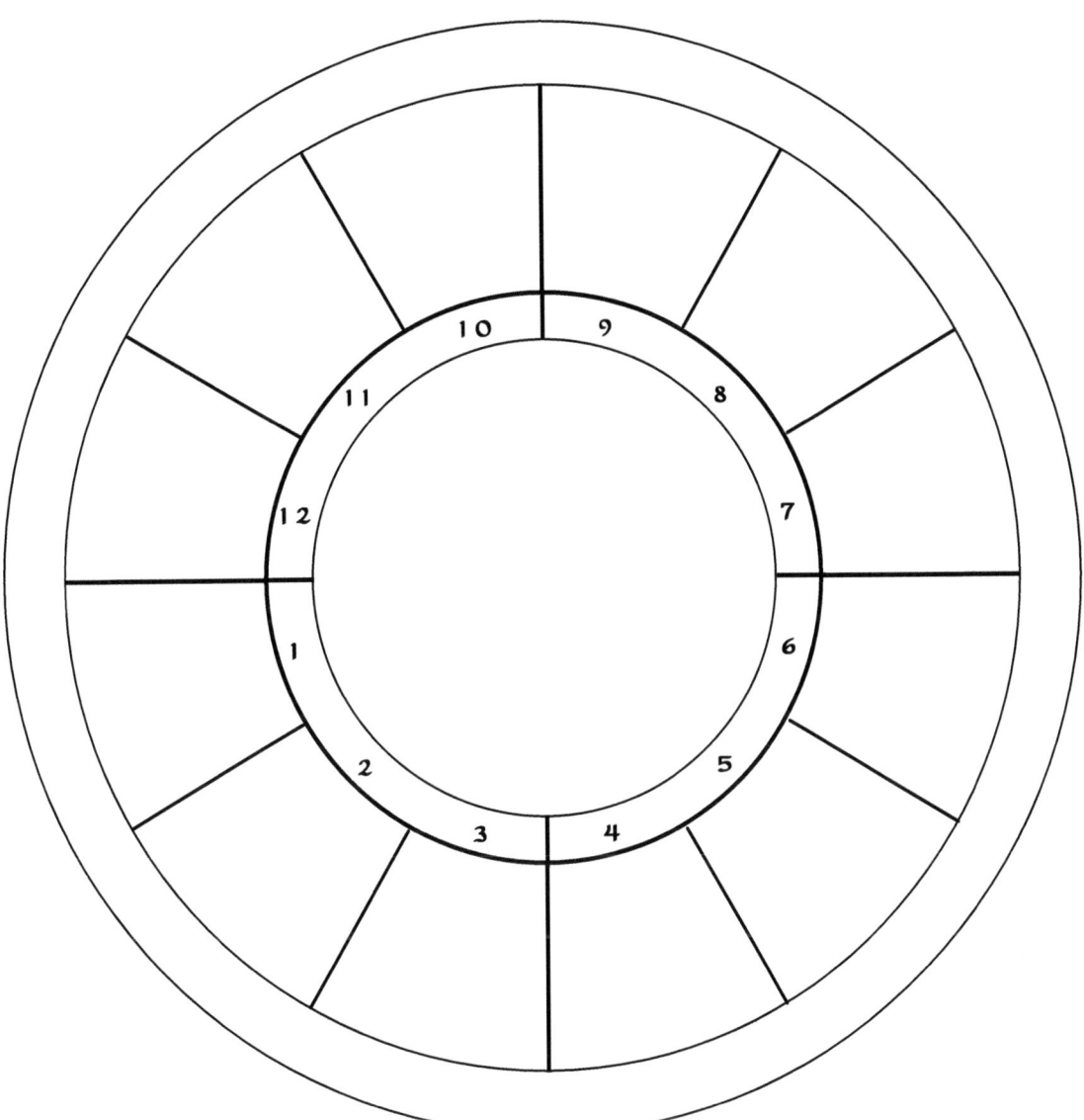

Planet	Position	Angle/Cusp	Position
☉		Ascendant (1st)	
☽		2nd House	
☿		3rd House	
♀		4th (IC)	
♂		5th House	
♃		6th House	
♄		7th (Descendant)	
♆		8th House	
♅		9th House	
♆		Midheaven (10th)	
♇		11th House	
☊		12th House	

12.

Part I: Fill In These Blanks (Look Up Information in Ephemeris and Atlas)

Name	Arnold Schwarzenegger	Time Zone Correction	CED (–2:00)
Date and Time of Birth	July 30, 1947 4:10 AM	Longitude Time Equivalent	–1:01:48
Location of Birth	Graz, Austria	Solar Sidereal Correction	0:21
Latitude & Longitude	47N05 15E27	Midnight Sidereal Time	20:27:09

Part II: Calculate the Constants You Will Need

Universal Time (UT) of Birth

Sidereal Time of Birth

Planet Travel (PT) (UT÷24 hrs)

Sidereal Differential

Latitude Differential

REMEMBER: Add 12 Hours to the Sidereal Time if Southern Hemisphere Chart!

Part III: Interpolate the Planets

Planet	Start	End	Total Travel	Travel x PT	Birth Position
☉	6♌00'05"	6♌57'26"			
☽	2♑27'09"	14♑16'35"			
☿	18♋00.3	18♋30.0			
♀	26♋15.3	27♋29.1			
♂	20♊02.7	20♊43.3			
♃	17♏59.4	18♏02.0			
♄	11♌34.3	11♌42.0			
⚷	3♏00.6	3♏03.7			
♅	24♊29.3	24♊32.1			
♆	8♎27.1	8♎28.3			
♇	12♌45.5	12♌47.3			
☊	0♊33.0 ℞	0♊26.0 ℞			

REMEMBER: If the planet is in Retrograde motion, SUBTRACT the Travel x PT from the Start Position to get the Birth Position!

Part IV: Interpolate the House Cusps

(Copy the Constants you will need from Page 1)

Sidereal Time of Birth _____

Sidereal Differential (SD) _____

Latitude Differential (LD) _____

Part IV(a): Calculate the Midheaven

Table 1 MC	Table 2 MC	Difference	Difference x SD	Natal MC
23♓28	24♓33			

Part IV(b): Calculate the Ascendant and the other House Cusps starting with the ADJUSTED Positions

Cusp	Table 1	Table 2	Difference	Difference x SD	Adjusted Cusp
Ascendant	18♋24	19♋11			
2nd	10♌31	11♌22			
3rd	1♍56	2♍54			
11th	17♉33	18♉36			
12th	23♊00	23♊50			

Part IV(c): Calculate the Final House Cusp Positions

Cusp	Table 1 Latitude 1	Table 1 Latitude 2	Difference	Difference x LD	Adjusted Cusp (Copy from Above)	ACTUAL HOUSE CUSP
ASC	18♋24	19♋11				
2nd	10♌31	11♌02				
3rd	1♍56	2♍12				
11th	17♉33	18♉46				
12th	23♊00	24♊05				

REMEMBER: If the signs are moving forward as you increase in Latitude, you ADD the Difference x LD to the Adjusted Cusp to find the Actual House Cusp. If the signs are moving backwards, you SUBTRACT the Difference x LD from the Adjusted Cusp to find the Actual House Cusp.

SOUTHERN HEMISPHERE CHARTS: Use the OPPOSITE SIGN of the Actual House Cusps as your final answer.

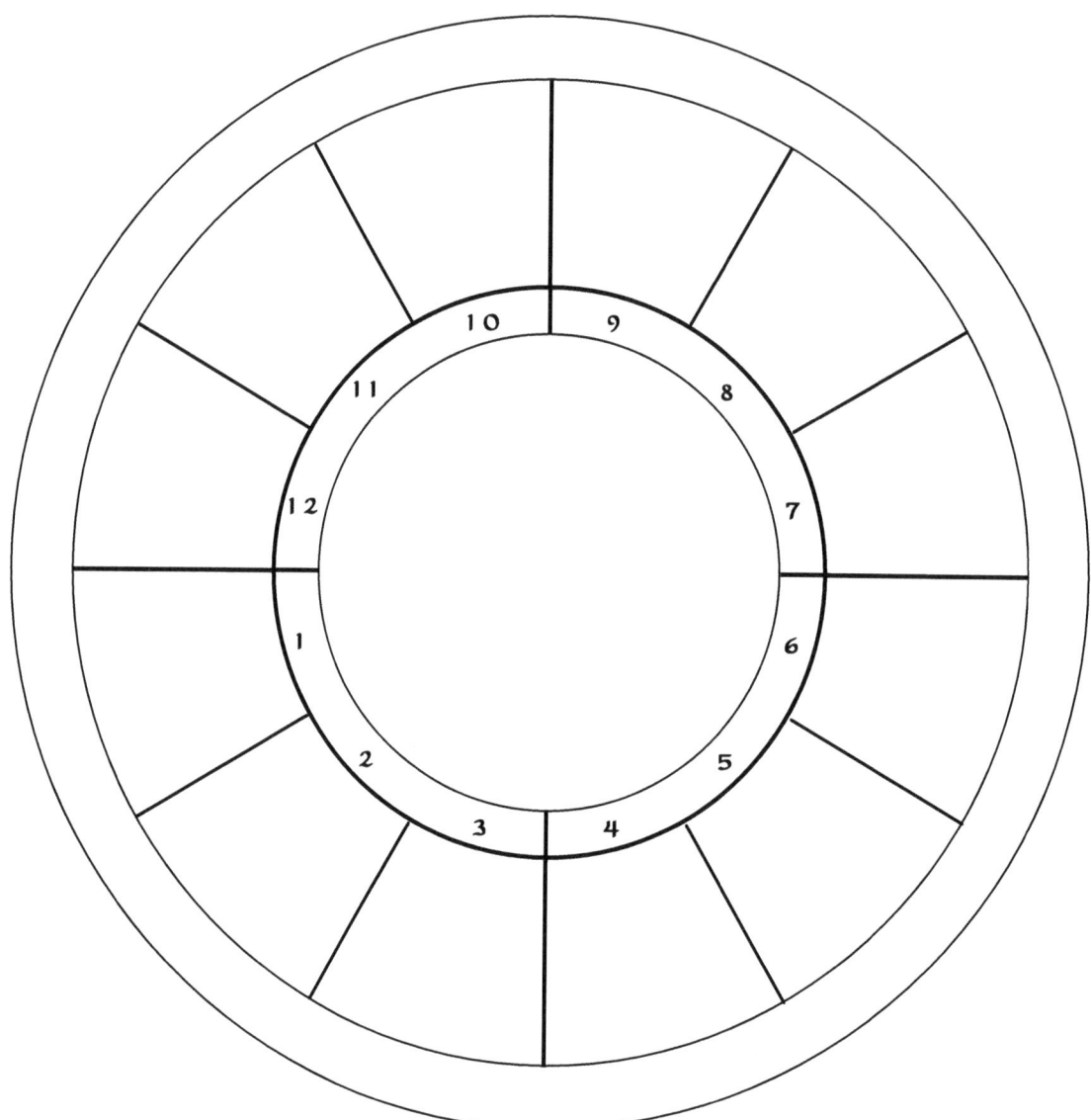

Planet	Position	Angle/Cusp	Position
☉		Ascendant (1st)	
☽		2nd House	
☿		3rd House	
♀		4th (IC)	
♂		5th House	
♃		6th House	
♄		7th (Descendant)	
♅		8th House	
♆		9th House	
♇		Midheaven (10th)	
⚷		11th House	
☊		12th House	

13.

Part I: Fill In These Blanks (Look Up Information in Ephemeris and Atlas)

Name	Evita Peron	Time Zone Correction	AROT (4:17)
Date and Time of Birth	May 7, 1919 5:00 AM	Longitude Time Equivalent	3:53:48
Location of Birth	Buenos Aires, Argentina	Solar Sidereal Correction	1:32
Latitude & Longitude	34S36 58W27	Midnight Sidereal Time	14:55:09

Part II: Calculate the Constants You Will Need

Universal Time (UT) of Birth _____

Sidereal Time of Birth _____

Planet Travel (PT) (UT÷24 hrs) _____

Sidereal Differential _____

Latitude Differential _____

REMEMBER: Add 12 Hours to the Sidereal Time if Southern Hemisphere Chart!

Part III: Interpolate the Planets

Planet	Start	End	Total Travel	Travel x PT	Birth Position
☉	15♉23'18"	16♉21'22"			
☽	15♌36'37"	28♌25'01"			
☿	18♈57.9	19♈59.9			
♀	23♊16.6	24♊26.5			
♂	16♉3.2	16♉46.8			
♃	11♋51.5	12♋1.6			
♄	21♌30.3	21♌31.8			
⚷	5♈17.6	5♈20.5			
♅	1♓19.1	1♓20.5			
♆	6♌37.5	6♌38.2			
♇	4♋58.9	4♋59.9			
☊	04♐0.3 ℞	03♐59.9 ℞			

REMEMBER: If the planet is in Retrograde motion, SUBTRACT the Travel x PT from the Start Position to get the Birth Position!

Part IV: Interpolate the House Cusps

(Copy the Constants you will need from Page 1)

Sidereal Time of Birth _____

Sidereal Differential (SD) _____

Latitude Differential (LD) _____

Part IV(a): Calculate the Midheaven

Table 1 MC	Table 2 MC	Difference	Difference x SD	Natal MC
1♌45	2♌43			

Part IV(b): Calculate the Ascendant and the other House Cusps starting with the ADJUSTED Positions

Cusp	Table 1	Table 2	Difference	Difference x SD	Adjusted Cusp
Ascendant	28♎31	29♎21			
2nd	27♏08	27♏55			
3rd	26♐41	27♐29			
11th	00♍21	01♍17			
12th	29♍26	00♎19			

Part IV(c): Calculate the Final House Cusp Positions

Cusp	Table 1 Latitude 1	Table 1 Latitude 2	Difference	Difference x LD	Adjusted Cusp (Copy from Above)	ACTUAL HOUSE CUSP
ASC	28♎31	28♎17				
2nd	27♏08	26♏50				
3rd	26♐41	26♐24				
11th	00♍21	00♍18				
12th	29♍26	29♍17				

REMEMBER: If the signs are moving forward as you increase in Latitude, you ADD the Difference x LD to the Adjusted Cusp to find the Actual House Cusp. If the signs are moving backwards, you SUBTRACT the Difference x LD from the Adjusted Cusp to find the Actual House Cusp.

SOUTHERN HEMISPHERE CHARTS: Use the OPPOSITE SIGN of the Actual House Cusps as your final answer.

Lesson 6: Interpolating the Angles and House Cusps

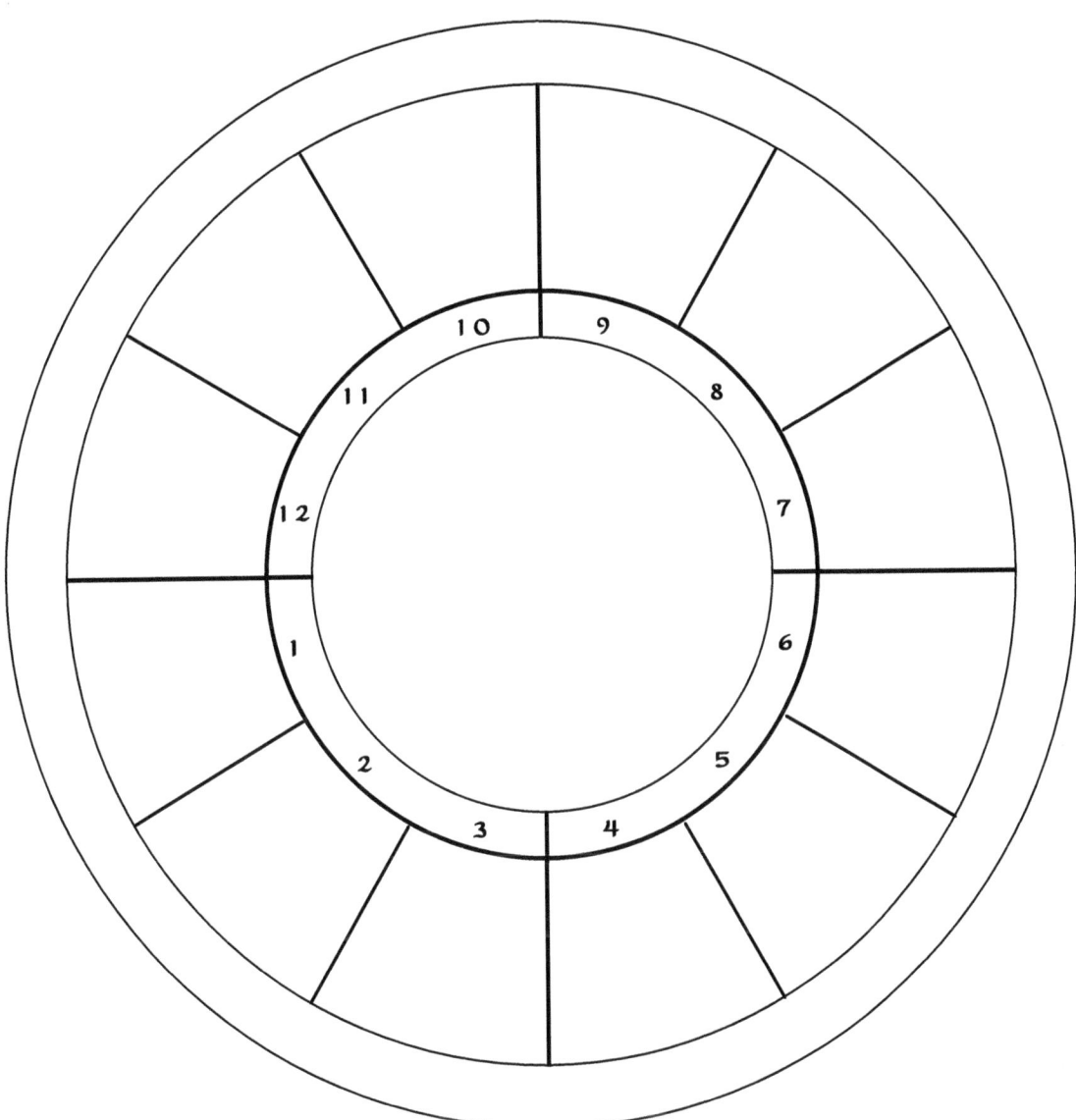

Planet	Position	Angle/Cusp	Position
☉		Ascendant (1st)	
☽		2nd House	
☿		3rd House	
♀		4th (IC)	
♂		5th House	
♃		6th House	
♄		7th (Descendant)	
⚷		8th House	
♅		9th House	
♆		Midheaven (10th)	
♇		11th House	
☊		12th House	

14.

Part I: Fill In These Blanks (Look Up Information in Ephemeris and Atlas)

Name	Rupert Murdoch	Time Zone Correction	AEST (–10:00)
Date and Time of Birth	March 11, 1931 11:59 PM	Longitude Time Equivalent	–9:39:52
Location of Birth	Melbourne, Australia	Solar Sidereal Correction	2:18
Latitude & Longitude	37S49 144E58	Midnight Sidereal Time	11:10:46

Part II: Calculate the Constants You Will Need

Universal Time (UT) of Birth

Sidereal Time of Birth

Planet Travel (PT) (UT÷24 hrs)

Sidereal Differential

Latitude Differential

REMEMBER: Add 12 Hours to the Sidereal Time if Southern Hemisphere Chart!

Part III: Interpolate the Planets

Planet	Start	End	Total Travel	Travel x PT	Birth Position
☉	19♓27'18"	20♓27'12"			
☽	16♐50'19"	29♐39'32"			
☿	14♓51.3	16♓44.1			
♀	5♒49.0	6♒57.9			
♂	27♋27.9	27♋30.0			
♃	10♋28.2	10♋29.1			
♄	21♑02.1	21♑06.9			
⚷	15♉04.2	15♉06.9			
♅	13♈52.3	13♈55.5			
♆	3♍59.9 ℞	3♍58.3 ℞			
♇	18♋47.5 ℞	18♋46.9 ℞			
☊	14♈40.2 ℞	14♈39.9 ℞			

REMEMBER: If the planet is in Retrograde motion, SUBTRACT the Travel x PT from the Start Position to get the Birth Position!

Part IV: Interpolate the House Cusps

(Copy the Constants you will need from Page 1)

Sidereal Time of Birth _____

Sidereal Differential (SD) _____

Latitude Differential (LD) _____

Part IV(a): Calculate the Midheaven

Table 1 MC	Table 2 MC	Difference	Difference x SD	Natal MC
10♓30	11♓34			

Part IV(b): Calculate the Ascendant and the other House Cusps starting with the ADJUSTED Positions

Cusp	Table 1	Table 2	Difference	Difference x SD	Adjusted Cusp
Ascendant	00♋59	01♋54			
2nd	25♋31	25♋57			
3rd	18♌01	18♌44			
11th	25♈08	26♈20			
12th	02♊31	03♊32			

Part IV(c): Calculate the Final House Cusp Positions

Cusp	Table 1 Latitude 1	Table 1 Latitude 2	Difference	Difference x LD	Adjusted Cusp (Copy from Above)	ACTUAL HOUSE CUSP
ASC	00♋59	01♋39				
2nd	25♋31	26♋00				
3rd	18♌01	18♌16				
11th	25♈08	25♈47				
12th	02♊31	03♊19				

REMEMBER: If the signs are moving forward as you increase in Latitude, you ADD the Difference x LD to the Adjusted Cusp to find the Actual House Cusp. If the signs are moving backwards, you SUBTRACT the Difference x LD from the Adjusted Cusp to find the Actual House Cusp.

SOUTHERN HEMISPHERE CHARTS: Use the OPPOSITE SIGN of the Actual House Cusps as your final answer.

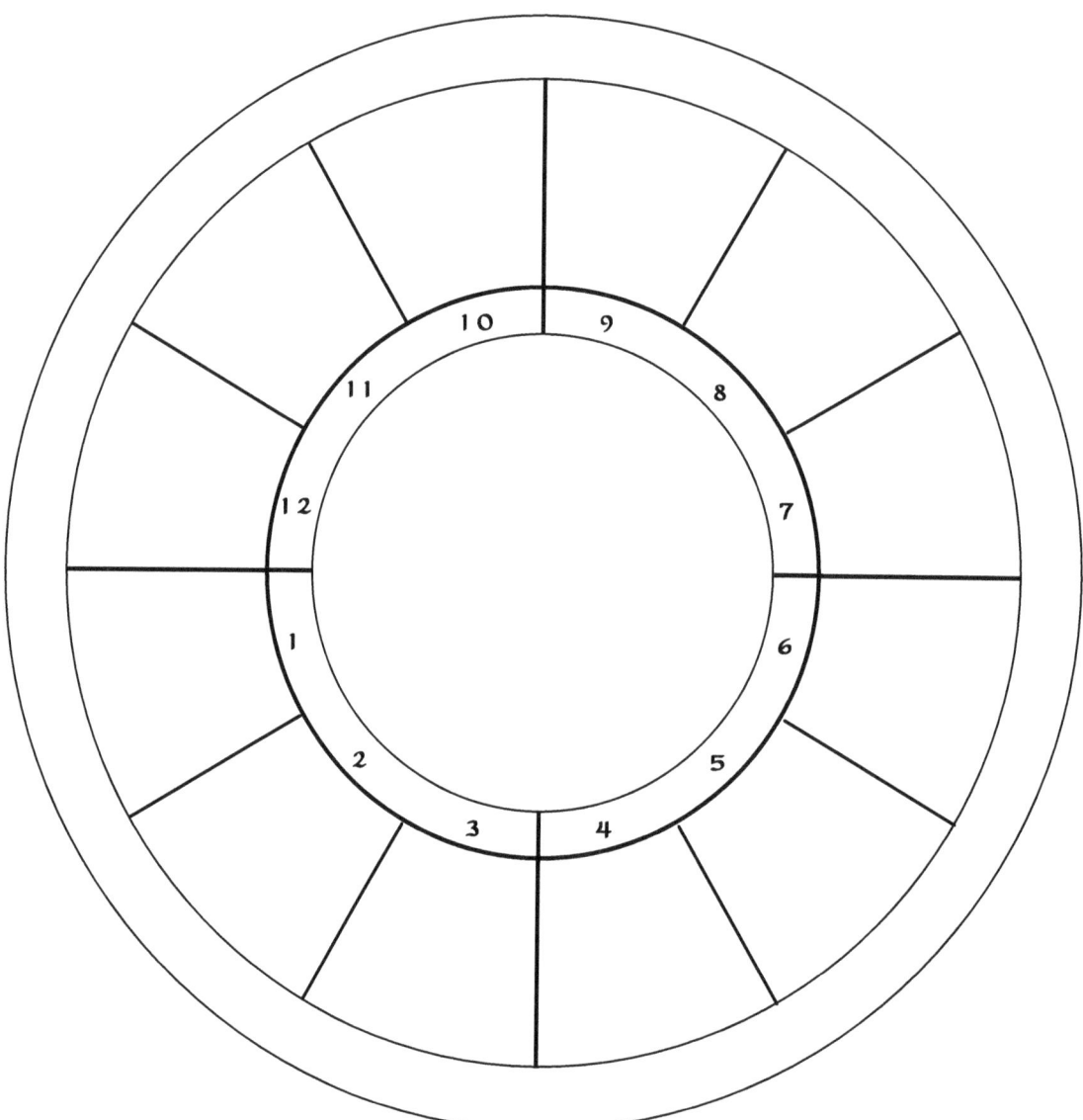

Planet	Position	Angle/Cusp	Position
☉		Ascendant (1st)	
☽		2nd House	
☿		3rd House	
♀		4th (IC)	
♂		5th House	
♃		6th House	
♄		7th (Descendant)	
♆		8th House	
♅		9th House	
♆		Midheaven (10th)	
♇		11th House	
☊		12th House	

Lesson 7: Relocation Charts

Many astrologers work with **relocated charts** and specialize in helping individuals to find what areas of the world will help emphasize the more easy and advantageous areas of the natal chart. Calculating a relocation chart is very easy, and uses the exact same information that we need for calculating a natal chart, with the addition of the **latitude, longitude,** and **Longitude Time Equivalent** for the new location.

The *only* difference between a relocated chart and a natal chart is the *houses. The longitudinal positions of the planets do not change in relocated charts.*

This bears repeating: *in a relocated chart, the planets stay at the exact same coordinates as in the natal chart.* The only changes are that the angles and house cusps (and therefore the relative placements of the planets around the chart) will change.

The quickest way to make sure that a relocated chart calculated by computer is correct, is to **check the position of the Moon in the relocated chart** and make sure it's exactly the same as the position of the Moon in the Natal Chart.

Calculating the Sidereal Time for the Relocated Chart

We calculate the **Sidereal Time** for a relocated chart in the same way as we do for a natal chart, with one very important exception. Instead of the **Longitude Time Equivalent** for the location of birth, we will use the **Longitude Time Equivalent** for the *new location*. This, of course, will give us an entirely different set of tables in the table of houses, and therefore an entirely different set of house cusps.

Using my chart as an example, I was born on October 24, 1967 at 9:47 P.M. CDT, in New Orleans, Louisiana. Let's relocate my chart to Honolulu, Hawaii. Here's how the information would look.

Name	Kevin Burk
Date and Time of Birth	October 24, 1967 9:47 PM
Location of Birth	New Orleans, LA
Latitude & Longitude	29N57'16" 90W23'16"
NEW Latitude & Longitude	21N18'25" 157W51'30"
Universal Time of Birth	October 25, 1967 02:47
Time Zone Correction	CDT (+5:00)
Longitude Time Equivalent	6:00:18 (New Orleans, LA)
Solar Sidereal Correction	0:27
Midnight Sidereal Time	2:10:47
NEW Longitude Time Equivalent	10:31:26 (Honolulu, HI)

Here's how we calculate the Relocated Sidereal Time.

	UT of Birth:	02:47:00		
+	Midnight Sidereal Time:	02:10:47		
		04:57:47		
+	Solar-Sidereal Correction (SSC):	00:00:27		
		04:57:74		28:57:74
−	*NEW Longitude Time Equivalent*	10:31:26	=	10:31:26
	RELOCATED SIDEREAL TIME:			18:26:48

Up until the last step, it's exactly the same as calculating the **Sidereal Time** for the Natal Chart.

We can now go to the **table of houses,** locate the tables that we need, calculate the SD and the LD (using the *relocated latitude,* remember!), and complete the relocated chart.

As always, if the chart is being relocated to the Southern Hemisphere, simply add 12 hours to the **Relocated Sidereal Time** (and adjust if needed to fit within the 0–24 hour range), and remember to use the opposite signs when you calculate the house cusps.

Exercises: Find the Relocated Sidereal Times

Relocate the charts for Meryl Streep, Arnold Schwarzenegger, Evita Peron and Rupert Murdoch to each of these four new cities: Los Angeles, California; Honolulu, Hawaii; Jakarta, Indonesia; and Paris, France. All of the information that you will need is listed below. Then match each **Relocated Sidereal Time** with the appropriate pair of **Sidereal Time Tables.** Remember to compensate for the Eastern and Southern Hemisphere locations!

Lesson 7: Relocation Charts

Name	UT of Birth	Solar-Sidereal Correction	Midnight Sidereal Time
Meryl Streep	12:05 GMT	01:59	17:59:23
Arnold Schwarzenegger	02:10 GMT	00:21	20:27:09
Evita Peron	09:17 GMT	01:32	14:55:09
Rupert Murdoch	13:59 GMT	02:18	11:10:46

City	Latitude	Longitude	Longitude Time Equivalent
Los Angeles, California	34N03	118W14	7:52:56
Honolulu, Hawaii	21N57	90W23	10:31:24
Jakarta, Indonesia	6S10	106E48	–07:07:12
Paris, France	48N52	2E20	–00:09:20

Name	Relocated To:	Answer:
Meryl Streep	Honolulu	
	Jakarta	
	Los Angeles	
	Paris	
Arnold Schwarzenegger	Honolulu	
	Jakarta	
	Los Angeles	
	Paris	
Evita Peron	Honolulu	
	Jakarta	
	Los Angeles	
	Paris	
Rupert Murdoch	Honolulu	
	Jakarta	
	Los Angeles	
	Paris	

	Sidereal Tables
A	0h 20m 0s – 0h 24m 0s
B	1h 12m 0s – 1h 16m 0s
C	1h 20m 0s – 1h 24m 0s
D	6h 12m 0s – 6h 16m 0s
E	12h 04m 0s – 12h 08m 0s
F	13h 40m 0s – 13h 44m 0s
G	14h 40m 0s – 14h 44m 0s
H	14h 44m 0s – 14h 48m 0s
I	16h 20m 0s – 16h 24m 0s
J	17h 16m 0s – 17h 20m 0s
K	17h 44m 0s – 17h 48m 0s
L	19h 20m 0s – 19h 24m 0s
M	19h 32m 0s – 19h 36m 0s
N	20h 16m 0s – 20h 20m 0s
O	22h 12m 0s – 22h 16m 0s
P	22h 44m 0s – 22h 48m 0s

Notes

Lesson 8:
Solar and Lunar Return Charts

Calculating **Solar and Lunar Return Charts** is exactly the same as calculating a Natal Chart. The only difference is that with the return charts, you first have to work backwards from the position of the Sun or Moon in order to find the actual **Universal Time and Date** for the return chart. Once you have that information, you simply use the Latitude, Longitude, and **Longitude Time Equivalent** from the **Atlas** for the location of the return chart, and interpolate the rest of the planets and the house cusps.

Solar Return Calculations

Let's take as an example my 1999 **Solar Return** for San Diego, California. We begin with the exact position of my Natal Sun (0♏59′55″) and look in the **Ephemeris** in October of 1999 to see what day the Sun will return to this position. We discover that the Sun will return to that position sometime between Midnight October 24, 1999 and Midnight October 25, 1999. Now, we already know the position of the Sun in my **Solar Return Chart**. What we don't know, however, is the **Universal Time** of that chart so that we can find the positions of the rest of the planets.

We can easily find this out by calculating the **PT** constant for the chart—the only difference is that we're going to work backwards. We will take the distance the Sun has traveled from Midnight October 24, 1999 to get to the natal Sun position, and divide it by the total distance that the Sun traveled from October 24, 1999 to October 25, 1999. This will give us the **PT** constant, which we can then use to interpolate the positions of the rest of the planets in the chart. Once we have the **PT** constant, we can easily use it to find the **UT** for the **Solar Return Chart** (which we will need to find the **Sidereal Time** and calculate the houses and angles). Here's how it looks using my chart. First let's find out how far the Sun traveled.

Natal Position of Sun:	0♏59′55″
− Sun at Midnight on October 24, 1999:	0♏07′47″
	52′08″ = 52.1333 minutes of arc

Next, we find out the total distance the Sun traveled.

Sun at Midnight on October 25, 1999	1♏07′32″	= 0♏66′92″
− Sun at Midnight on October 24, 1999:	0♏07′47″	= 0♏07′47″
		59′45″ = 59.75 minutes

We divide 52.1333 minutes by 59.75 minutes to come up with the PT constant of 0.8725.

Finding the Universal Time (GMT) of the Return Chart

Once we have the PT constant for the **Solar Return Chart,** finding the UT of the chart is simply a matter of multiplying the PT by 24 hours and converting the result back into hours, minutes and seconds. In this case, we take 24 hours x the PT of 0.8725 and get 20.94 hours, which converts back into 20:56:24 UT. (For a review of how to convert from a decimal back into hours, minutes, and seconds, see Chapter 3.)

Lunar Return Calculations

The calculations involved in a **Lunar Return** are identical to those in a **Solar Return.** The only real difference is that **Lunar Returns** occur thirteen times a year, and we'll be solving for the position of the Moon, not of the Sun. Let's take a look at my first October, 1999 **Lunar Return,** which according to the **Ephemeris** will occur sometime between Midnight on October 2, 1999 and Midnight on October 3, 1999. (There will be another **Lunar Return** before the end of October as well, because the period between **Lunar Returns** is only about 27⅓ days.)

As always, we start out by finding out how far the Moon traveled from the Midnight position on the earlier date, to the Natal Position of the Moon.

Natal Position of Moon:	14♋39′36″
− Moon at Midnight on October 2, 1999:	6♋09′36″
	8° 30′00″ = 8.5 degrees

Next, we look at the total distance the Moon traveled from October 2 to October 3.

Moon at Midnight on October 3, 1999	20♋07′03″	= 19♋66′63″
− Moon at Midnight on October 2, 1999:	6♋09′36″	= 6♋09′36″
		13°57′27″ = 13.9575 degrees

We divide 8.5 degrees by 13.9575 degrees to find the PT of 0.6090.
Finally, we multiply the PT by 24 hours to find the UT of the return.

0.6090 x 24 hours = 14.6158 hours =
14 hours 36.9478 minutes = 14:36:57 UT of Return.

Exercises: Find the UT of the Return Charts

Natal Position	Date 1 Position	Date 2 Position	PT	UT of Return
1. 16♐21'13"	15♐25'56"	16♐26'53"		
2. 4♓59'46"	28♒25'41"	11♓49'08"		
3. 29♊40'24"	19♊14'38"	4♋32'19"		
4. 12♈10'52"	11♈34'03"	12♈33'16"		
5. 3♒02'11"	2♒16'21"	3♒17'22"		

Precession Corrected Return Charts

In addition to basic **return charts,** many astrologers, myself included, work primarily with **precession-corrected return charts.** Because of the wobble of the Earth's axis, there exists an ever-increasing discrepancy between the positions of the **Tropical Zodiac** (used by the vast majority of Western Astrologers) and the **Sidereal Zodiac** (used primarily in Eastern Astrological practices) which is based on the positions of the Fixed Stars. The Spring Equinox, which is 0° Aries in the Tropical Zodiac, occurs at a slightly earlier point each year along the Sidereal Zodiac. This phenomenon of slipping backwards is called **precession**, and it occurs at a rate of 1° every 71½ years (which translates to approximately 4 seconds of arc each month).

Precession-corrected return charts do not use the natal positions of the planets as the return point; instead, they take into account the amount of precession that has occurred from the date of birth to the date of the return chart, and base the return chart on this revised position of the Sun or Moon. Once the precessed positions are found, calculating the rest of the chart works exactly the same way as for a non-precessed return chart. Again, the only difference between the two is that **precession-corrected returns will be calculated for a position different from the natal planet's position—a position that will change slightly from year to year.** To determine exactly how much precession we need to take into account, we need to look at the **Synetic Vernal Point (SVP)** listings in the Ephemeris.

The Synetic Vernal Point (SVP)

The **Synetic Vernal Point** or **SVP**, is listed in the "Astro Data" column on the bottom of each page of the ephemeris. The SVP is listed for the first day of each month. The coordinates listed for the SVP are the Sidereal Equivalent on that date, for 0° Aries in the Tropical Zodiac.

Synetic Vernal Point (SVP)
Listed for the First Day of Each Month

Astro Data	Planet Ingress	Last Aspect	☽ Ingress	Last Aspect	☽ Ingress	☽ Phases & Eclipses	Astro Data
Dy Hr Mn	Dy Hr Mn	Dy Hr Mn	Dy Hr Mn	Dy Hr Mn	Dy Hr Mn	Dy Hr Mn	1 OCTOBER 1967
☽0S 3 12:13	♀ ♍ 1 18:07	1 3:14 ♀ ☌	♍ 1 3:38	31 2:47 ♄ ☍	♏ 1 15:26	3 20:24 ● 9♎56	Julian Day # 24745
☽0N 16 18:38	♃ ♍ 19 10:51	2 21:43 ♅ ☌	♎ 3 4:34	3 10:55 ♅ ⚹	♐ 3 14:51	10 12:11 ☽ 16♑30	Delta T 38.1 sec
♄♇♆ 16 18:07	♂ ♑ 23 2:14	5 0:13 ♃ ⚹	♏ 5 4:14	5 11:47 ♅ □	♑ 5 15:44	18 10:11 ○ 24♈21	SVP 05♓42'45"
☿ R 21 5:15	☉ ♏ 24 2:44	7 1:00 ♃ □	♐ 7 4:32	7 16:09 ♀ △	♒ 7 19:45	18 10:15 ☍T 1.143	Obliquity 23°26'45"
☽0S 30 23:19		9 3:59 ♃ △	♑ 9 7:04	9 15:50 ♆ □	♓ 10 3:42	26 12:04 ☾ 2♌23	⚷ Chiron 27♓05.1R
	♀ ♎ 9 16:32	11 5:50 ♅ △	♒ 11 12:45	12 10:52 ♅ ☍	♈ 12 14:58		☽ Mean ☊ 28♈51.8
☿ D 10 16:16	☉ ♐ 23 0:04	13 19:47 ♃ ☍	♓ 13 21:38	14 0:05 ♂ □	♉ 15 3:52	2 5:48 ● 9♏07	
♀0S 12 3:36		16 1:59 ♅ ☍	♈ 16 8:58	17 13:00 ♅ △	♊ 17 16:40	2 5:38:17 ☌T non-C	1 NOVEMBER 1967
☽0N 13 0:37		18 21:30 ♃ △	♉ 18 21:41	20 0:51 ♅ □	♋ 20 4:13	9 1:00 ☽ 15♒56	Julian Day # 24776
♄0S 18 9:03		21 4:12 ♅ △	♊ 21 10:38	22 12:54 ☉ △	♌ 22 13:47	17 4:53 ○ 24♉09	Delta T 38.1 sec
☽0S 27 8:37		23 22:04 ☉ △	♋ 23 22:27	24 10:38 ♆ □	♍ 24 20:46	25 0:23 ☾ 2♍02	SVP 05♓42'42"
		26 2:16 ♅ ⚹	♌ 26 7:40	26 22:20 ♅ ☌	♎ 27 0:48		Obliquity 23°26'45"
		28 1:44 ♆ □	♍ 28 13:19	28 22:37 ♂ □	♏ 29 2:13		⚷ Chiron 25♓52.6R
		30 11:09 ♅ ☌	♎ 30 15:31				☽ Mean ☊ 27♈13.3

The amount of precession is the difference between the SVP listed for the individual's birth date (on the 1st of the month), and the SVP listed for the 1st of the month of the return chart. Subtract the current SVP from the natal SVP, and you have the amount of precession. Add this to the Natal position of the Sun and/or Moon, and you're ready to calculate the **precession-corrected solar or lunar return chart.** Let's take my chart as an example, and determine the amount of precession for my 1999 **Solar Return.**

Natal SVP:	5♓ 42′45″
– Return SVP:	5♓ 16′02″
PRECESSION:	26′ 43″

We then add this amount to my natal Sun's position, and come up with the position of the Sun for the **precession-corrected return chart.**

Natal Sun Position:	0♏59′ 55″
+ Precession:	26′ 43″
Precession-Corrected Sun:	1♏26′ 38″

Quarti-Returns and Demi-Returns

We can also apply the same calculation techniques to any kind of return chart, including **harmonic return charts.** The most common harmonic return charts are the 4th harmonic return charts which include the **Quarti-Return** (quarter), **Demi-Return** (half), and **Triquarti-Return** (three-quarters). These returns are simply calculated for the 4th harmonic positions from the natal position. In other words, since my natal Sun is at 0♏59′55″, then my **quarti-return** position would be 0♒59′55″ (the waxing square to the natal position), my **demi-return** position is 0♉59′55″ (the opposition to the natal position), and my **tri-quarti-return** position is 0♌59′55″ (which is the waning square to the natal position). These returns can be corrected for precession in the same way as for full returns: simply calculate the difference between the SVP's of the birth date and the date of the return chart and add the difference to the return position.

Lesson 9: Secondary Progressions

Secondary progressions are a symbolic predictive technique that works with the natal chart, and takes each day after birth to correspond to one year of life for the individual. **Progressions** are generally used to show trends for the year, and are usually interpreted to relate to a person's inner life, as opposed to external events. The progressed Moon is often an important timing factor in predictive astrology. In most methods of **secondary progression,** not a lot of activity is evident in the chart because the progressed planets move at such an exceedingly slow pace, and in general, it's the changes (by sign, aspect, house, or direction) in the progressed chart that are important from an interpretation standpoint. Thanks to the recommendations of Jim Shawvan, a colleague of mine in San Diego, and a rather accomplished predictive and relocation astrologer, I've personally started to work with the **Quotidian** (Latin for daily) method of **secondary progressions,** where the houses and angles move at a relatively rapid pace. I've found this method to be quite effective as a predictive technique for external events, with the timing of the events correlating to the aspects between the angles and house cusps to the progressed planets and/or natal planets and cusps.

Finding the Progressed Dates in the Ephemeris

Secondary progressions are based on the idea that each day after birth is equivalent to one year of life for the individual. In order to find what dates to use in the ephemeris in order to calculate the positions of the progressed planets, we simply start counting from the day after the UT date of birth until we reach the date that corresponds to the individual's current age. In my case, my UT date of birth is October 25, 1967. As I'm writing this, in June of 1999, I'm currently 31 years old. So, starting with October 26, 1967 in the **ephemeris**, and counting forward for 31 days, we come up with the date of November 25, 1967, which would then correspond to my progressed planets for the 31st year of my life.

Now I'm more than half-way through the year, and with progressions, minutes do count, particularly when we're looking at the Sun and Moon. So actually, my progressed planets would fall somewhere between the positions listed at Midnight on November 25, 1967, and Midnight on

November 26, 1967, and in order to find the actual positions on any given day of the year, we'll need to interpolate between the two dates.

Although the actual interpolation is identical to interpolating the positions of natal planets, we're going to need to use a different set of constants because we're not dealing with a 24-hour period *per se*—we're actually dealing with an entire year. We can't simply use the Midnight GMT listings of the planets in the ephemeris as our reference point, because the "time" of the progressed chart changes every day. We need to find a more reliable anchor—a reference point where we can use the listed ephemeris data as is. This is called the **Adjusted Calculation Date.**

The Adjusted Calculation Date

The **Adjusted Calculation Date (ACD)** is the date each year when the midnight positions of the planets listed in the ephemeris for the given progressed day/year correspond exactly to the positions of the progressed planets in the chart. If you only calculated one progressed chart for yourself each year, always on the date of your individual **ACD**, you wouldn't ever have to interpolate the positions of the planets.

Finding the **ACD** is relatively simple, although it does require an Ephemeris. Look up the **Midnight Sidereal Time** listed in the Ephemeris for the **UT** of Birth (make sure you use the date of the **UT**!). Then subtract the **UT** of birth from the **Midnight Sidereal Time** listed in the Ephemeris. Take this result, and going backwards in the Ephemeris listings from the date of birth, look for the date that matches this new **Midnight Sidereal Time.** This date is the **Adjusted Calculation Date** for the individual.

Once again, we'll use my chart as an example. My **UT** of birth is 2:47 GMT, October 25, 1967, and the **Midnight Sidereal Time** listed in the Ephemeris for this date is 2:10:47.

Midnight Sidereal Time	2:10:47	= 1:70:47	= 25:70:47
UT of Birth	2:47	= 2:47	= 2:47
ACD Sidereal Time			**23:23:47**

Remember that with **Sidereal Time,** since the stars don't care about the local time and date, if we need to add 24 hours in order to be able to subtract the **UT**, we can do so easily.

Looking up the **ACD Sidereal Time** in the ephemeris, we find the closest match to be on September 12, 1967, when the **Midnight Sidereal Time** is listed as 23:21:15, so my **ACD** is September 12 of each year.

Calculating the Progressed Planet Travel (PPT) Constant

Now that we know the **ACD**, we have a fixed reference point that lets us measure how far along the 365-day year we are. We can use this date to help us to calculate the **Progressed Planet Travel (PPT)** Constant which we will use to interpolate the planetary positions in the progressed chart in the same way as we used the **Planet Travel (PT)** Constant to interpolate the planetary positions in the natal chart.

Secondary progressions are a predictive technique, and therefore, are based on a specific date, in the same way that **transits** and **return charts** are based on a specific date. Where this date falls with respect to the 365-day period from one ACD to the next ACD will give us the PPT (again, in exactly the same way as where the UT of birth falls within the 24-hour period from Midnight on the date of birth to Midnight on the following date gives us the PT).

Once again, we will have to do some converting in order to make these calculations. We need to be able to convert both dates (the ACD and the **Progress-to-Date**) from Month and Day into **Julian Days** (which run from 1 (January 1) through 365 (December 31)). What we will then do is subtract the ACD from the **Progress-to-Date** (usually the current date), and divide this by the number of days in the year (365, or 366 in a leap year) to find the PPT constant.

On the next page is a quick reference table that will help you to easily convert dates into **Julian Days.**

Once again, to calculate the PPT constant, we **subtract the ACD from the Progress-to-Date and divide the result by the number of days in the year** (usually 365, or 366 during a leap year). If the year is a leap year, don't forget to compensate for that fact when you look up the Julian dates!

My ACD is September 12 of each year, which in Julian terms is Day 255. If I wanted to progress my chart to June 25, 1999 (the **Progress-to-Date** in this example), I'll first have to convert this date into **Julian days** (Day 176) and then subtract the ACD from this number. If it turns out that we're going to be subtracting a larger number from a smaller number (as is the case here), we simply "borrow a year" and add 365 to the smaller number and then subtract.

Progress-to-Date	176	[+365] =	541
– ACD	255	=	255
Difference in Days			286

We then divide this number by 365 days in the year (1999), and come up with the PPT of 0.7836. This is the constant that we will use to interpolate the positions of the planets between the two progressed dates that we found at the beginning of this exercise (November 25, 1967 and November 26, 1967).

CALENDAR DATES TO JULIAN DATES

	Jan	Feb	Mar	Apr	May	Jun	Jul	Aug	Sep	Oct	Nov	Dec
1	1	32	60	91	121	152	182	213	244	274	305	335
2	2	33	61	92	122	153	183	214	245	275	306	336
3	3	34	62	93	123	154	184	215	246	276	307	337
4	4	35	63	94	124	155	185	216	247	277	308	338
5	5	36	64	95	125	156	186	217	248	278	309	339
6	6	37	65	96	126	157	187	218	249	279	310	340
7	7	38	66	97	127	158	188	219	250	280	311	341
8	8	39	67	98	128	159	189	220	251	281	312	342
9	9	40	68	99	129	160	190	221	252	282	313	343
10	10	41	69	100	130	161	191	222	253	283	314	344
11	11	42	70	101	131	162	192	223	254	284	315	345
12	12	43	71	102	132	163	193	224	255	285	316	346
13	13	44	72	103	133	164	194	225	256	286	317	347
14	14	45	73	104	134	165	195	226	257	287	318	348
15	15	46	74	105	135	166	196	227	258	288	319	349
16	16	47	75	106	136	167	197	228	259	289	320	350
17	17	48	76	107	137	168	198	229	260	290	321	351
18	18	49	77	108	138	169	199	230	261	291	322	352
19	19	50	78	109	139	170	200	231	262	292	323	353
20	20	51	79	110	140	171	201	232	263	293	324	354
21	21	52	80	111	141	172	202	233	264	294	325	355
22	22	53	81	112	142	173	203	234	265	295	326	356
23	23	54	82	113	143	174	204	235	266	296	327	357
24	24	55	83	114	144	175	205	236	267	297	328	358
25	25	56	84	115	145	176	206	237	268	298	329	359
26	26	57	85	116	146	177	207	238	269	299	330	360
27	27	58	86	117	147	178	208	239	270	300	331	361
28	28	59	87	118	148	179	209	240	271	301	332	362
29	29	NOTE	88	119	149	180	210	241	272	302	333	363
30	30		89	120	150	181	211	242	273	303	334	364
31	31		90		151		212	243		304		365

NOTE: If it is a Leap Year, add "1" to every number from this point on!

© 2004 Kevin B. Burk — www.TheRealAstrology.com

Exercises: Calculate the PPT

	Progress-To-Date	ACD	Difference	PPT
1.	May 23, 1995	March 18		
2.	September 6, 1980	July 4		
3.	March 5, 1997	October 25		
4.	November 29, 1973	April 18		
5.	February 1, 1992	December 6		

NOTE: Make sure that you adjust for Leap Years when applicable! If there is a February 29th between the ACD preceding the **Progress-to-Date** and the ACD following a year later, divide by 366 days.

Calculate the Solar Arc

The next thing that we have to do is to calculate the **Solar Arc**. The **Solar Arc** is the difference between the position of the **Progressed Sun** and the **Natal Sun,** and will be used to help calculate the progressed house cusps and angles. In order to do this, we first need to find the position of the progressed Sun. This is a simple interpolation process using the **PPT** constant.

Sun on November 26, 1967:	3♐01'49"
Sun on November 25, 1967:	2♐01'07"
Distance Traveled:	1° 00'42" = 60.7'
Distance Traveled x PPT:	60.7' x 0.7836 = 47.5645' = 47'34"
Progressed Sun Position:	2♐01'07" + 47'34" = **2♐48'41"**

We then calculate the **Solar Arc** by subtracting the Natal Sun position from the Progressed Sun position.

Progressed Sun Position:	2♐ 48' 41" =	32♏ 48' 41" =	31♏ 107' 101"
− Natal Sun Position:	0♏ 59' 55" =	0♏ 59' 55" =	0♏ 59' 55"
		SOLAR ARC:	31 48' 46"

Calculating the House Cusps—Three Different Methods

When it comes to calculating the angles and houses for progressed charts, you have several different options. Each option is entirely valid from a mathematical standpoint, and if you're only looking to be able to pass the math portion of a certification exam, by all means, choose the simplest and quickest methods of calculating the houses. The two simple methods, however (**Solar Arc Directed Midheaven**, and **Meridian Arc Directed Midheaven**) will produce static progressed charts that tend to be less than useful as predictive tools. The third method (**Quotidian** or **Daily Progressions**) is a little more involved from a calculation standpoint, but it will produce progressed charts that can be used to help in timing and predictions.

In each case, we will work backwards with the math to come up with the interpolation constants that we will need, and then use these constants to interpolate the remaining house cusp positions (in much the same way as we worked backwards to find the time and dates of the return charts).

Solar Arc Directed Midheaven

The **Solar Arc** method of **secondary progressions** adds the **Solar Arc** to the position of the natal Midheaven to find the Progressed Midheaven. We then take the Progressed Midheaven position and look it up in the table of houses to find the two tables that we will use to calculate the remaining house cusps. We need to find the **Sidereal Differential** (SD) for these calculations, and we'll do this by using the Midheaven Positions. We'll divide the difference between the Progressed Midheaven and the Table 1 Midheaven by the total distance between the Table 1 Midheaven and the Table 2 Midheaven. Let's use my chart as an example, and find the progressed Midheaven for June 25, 1999 using the **Solar Arc** method.

Natal Midheaven Position:	13♓10	
+ Solar Arc:	31° 49′	
Progressed Midheaven:	44♓59′ =	14♈59′

In the **Koch Table of Houses**, we find that the closest Midheavens listed are 14♈07 (0h 52m 0s) and 15♈12 (0h 56m 0s).

Midheaven Table #2:	15♈12
− Midheaven Table #1:	14♈07
Total Distance:	1° 05′ = 65′
Progressed Midheaven:	14♈59′
− Midheaven Table #1:	14♈07
Difference:	52′

We divide the difference by the total distance and come up with the **Sidereal Differential** (SD) like so:

$$52' \div 65' = 0.8000 \text{ SD}$$

The **Latitude Differential** (LD) will, of course, depend on the location used for the progressed chart, and is calculated exactly the same way as it is for a natal chart.

We now have all of the information needed to calculate the rest of the progressed houses.

NOTE: If the natal chart being used is a **Southern Hemisphere Chart**, remember **to look up the opposite sign of the progressed Midheaven in the table of houses** (assuming you're using a **Northern Hemisphere** table of houses)! If my chart was a Southern Hemisphere Chart, we would have looked up the tables that corresponded to a Midheaven of 14♎59′, instead of for 14♈59′. And of course, once we calculated the remaining house cusps, we would have to use the opposite signs for the final answer, just as when calculating a natal chart in the Southern Hemisphere.

Meridian Arc Directed Midheaven

The **Meridian Arc Directed** method progresses the natal Midheaven by the individual's age at the date of the progressed chart, rather than by the **Solar Arc**. Each year corresponds to 1° of arc added to the natal Midheaven. Of course, if we want to be precise about the whole thing, we'll need to convert the number of days into the current year (from birthday to birthday) into additional minutes and seconds of arc. Again, we'll work from the UT date of birth, my natal chart, and progress the chart to June 25, 1999.

We need to convert the dates to **Julian days** just as we did when we calculated the ACD. In this case, however, the dates we need are the UT date of birth and the **Progress-to-Date,** and the number we're looking for is the difference between the date of birth and the progressed date.

Progress-to-Date:	June 25, 1999	176	[+365] =	541
− UT Birth Date:	Oct. 25 1967	298	=	298
Difference in Days				243

And just as when calculating the ACD, we'll divide this difference by the total number of days in the year (365) and come up with a percentage decimal (243 ÷ 365 = 0.6658). This is the number of minutes expressed in terms of *degrees*, and we simply convert it back into minutes by multiplying by 60 to get 39.9452 minutes, or 40 minutes. Adding the 31° for my current age to this, we get the **Meridian Arc** of 31°40′. And we get the progressed Midheaven position by adding this number to the natal Midheaven.

Natal Midheaven Position:	13♓ 10		
+ Meridian Arc:	31° 40′		
Progressed Midheaven:	44♓ 50′	= 14♈50′	

Notice how the two different methods come up with very similar results?

To calculate the rest of the houses, follow the same procedure as you would for a **Solar Arc Directed Midheaven.** Look up the progressed Midheaven in the table of houses to find the closest two table listings, interpolate between them to come up with the **SD**, and calculate the rest of the houses for the Latitude of the progressed chart.

Quotidian (Daily) Progressions

The **Quotidian** method of progressions takes into account the fact that during the course of the 24-hour day, the Midheaven doesn't cover just 1° of arc—it actually moves through about 361° of arc. The other methods of progressions only look at the net difference in the daily positions of the Midheaven. The **Quotidian** method looks at the actual daily motion of the house cusps and angles. And to be able to calculate the **Quotidian** progressed houses, we have to be able to figure out the exact derived time for the progressed chart.

How do we do this? Exactly the same way as we figure out the **UT** for a **Solar Return Chart.** Actually, this process is several steps shorter, because we already know what percentage of the day has elapsed—it's the **Progressed Planet Travel** (**PPT**) constant. Even though we calculated this number as the relationship between the number of days elapsed after the **ACD** and the number of days in the year, this number is also the relationship between the **UT** of the chart and the 24-hour day. We can find the derived **UT** of the progressed chart by simply multiplying the **PPT** by 24 hours.

In my case, we take the **PPT** of 0.7863 x 24 hours and get 18.8712 hours **UT**, and converting this back into a more conventional time format, we get a derived **UT** of 18:52:16.

Using the derived **UT** and date for the progressed chart (the **UT** we just calculated, for the derived progressed date which we obtained by counting one day for each year), and the location for the progressed chart, we can calculate the houses and angles as we would for a basic natal chart.

In my case, progressing my natal chart to June 25, 1999, the derived **UT** for the chart is November 25, 1967, 18:52:16 GMT. The progressed chart is the same as a natal chart for this date and time. Look up the **Solar-Sidereal Correction** and **Midnight Sidereal Time** using this time and date, and use the **Longitude Time Equivalent** from the **Atlas** for the location of the progressed chart to calculate the Sidereal Time for the chart. The **progressed chart** is usually done for the birthplace, but may also be done for the individual's current place or residence, or some location where they have lived or may want to live. Interpolating the houses and angles is straightforward from this point.

If the chart is being progressed to a location in the Southern Hemisphere, follow the same procedure as when calculating a Southern Hemisphere Natal Chart: add 12 hours to the **Sidereal Time,** and use the opposite signs for the final house cusp positions.

NOTE: As always, the conversions for Southern Hemisphere charts are assuming that the table of houses you are using is calculated for the Northern Hemisphere.

If you are using a **Southern Hemisphere Table of Houses,** you do not need to make any changes to Southern Hemisphere charts; **for** *Northern Hemisphere* **charts, you will need to** *subtract* **12 hours from the Sidereal Time and reverse the sign cusps.**

Notes

Lesson 10:
The Part of Fortune, the Vertex and the Equatorial Ascendant

This chapter covers how to calculate three additional points in the chart: the **Part of Fortune** (Fortuna), the **Vertex**, and the **Equatorial Ascendant**.

Calculating the Part of Fortune (and the Part of Spirit)

The **Part of Fortune**, also known as Fortuna, is a mathematically calculated point. It is one of many Arabic "Parts" (or Greek "Lots") that are calculated by comparing the arc distance between three points in the chart. The **Part of Fortune** is calculated differently depending on whether the chart is **Diurnal** (day chart, i.e., the Sun above the horizon in houses 12–7) or **Nocturnal** (night chart, i.e., the Sun below the horizon in houses 1–6).

>   Diurnal Chart: Ascendant + Moon – Sun
>   Nocturnal Chart: Ascendant + Sun – Moon

So what the heck does this mean? Well, it helps if you work backwards in the formulas. Taking the **Diurnal Chart** formula, it means that the distance from the Sun to the Moon (in degrees) is the same as the distance from the Ascendant to the **Part of Fortune**. The degrees are always measured through the signs (counter-clockwise around the chart).

The **Part of Fortune** and the **Part of Spirit** are only two of hundreds of Arabic "Parts" (also known in Classical Greek Astrology as "Lots"). Although the formulas for these points vary, they are usually expressed in the same way—that is, as "Point A + Point B – Point C." Simply follow the same procedure as you do when calculating the **Part of Fortune** or the **Part of Spirit** and work backwards, starting with the arc from Point C to Point B, and then apply that arc from Point A to find the Part or Lot in question.

The formula for the **Part of Spirit** (by the way) is the inverse of the formula for the **Part of Fortune**.

>   Diurnal Chart: Ascendant + Sun – Moon
>   Nocturnal Chart: Ascendant + Moon – Sun.

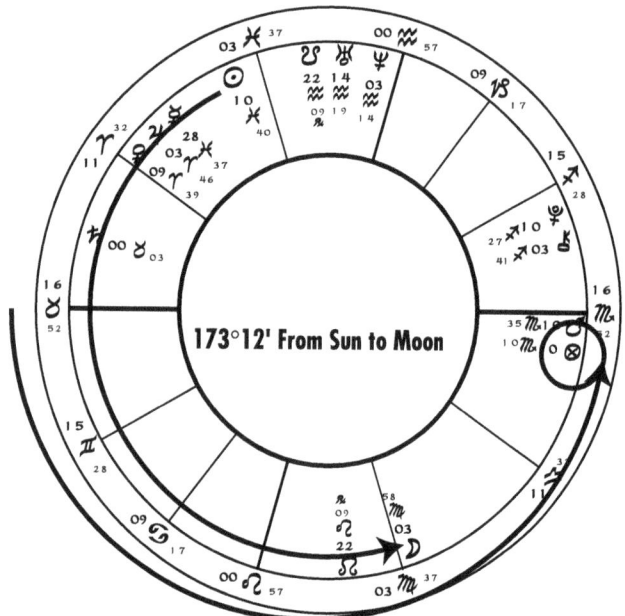
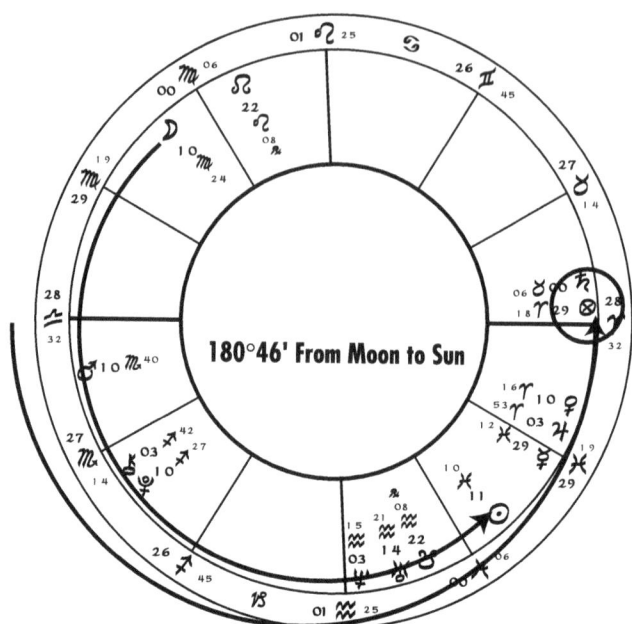

173°12' From Ascendant to Part of Fortune

180°46' From Ascendant to Part of Fortune

Calculating the Part of Fortune in a Diurnal Chart:
Ascendant + Moon − Sun

Calculating the Part of Fortune in a Nocturnal Chart:
Ascendant + Sun − Moon

Calculating the Vertex

The **Vertex** is the intersection of the **Prime Vertical** and the **Ecliptic** in the West. The **Vertex** is thought to operate as a kind of an unconscious descendant, and to represent the qualities that we find desirable in a partner on an unconscious level. Relationships that connect with the **Vertex** often seem to have a "fated" quality about them. The **Vertex** may also operate as a pressure valve in the chart—the point where things tend to explode. I've personally seen the **Vertex** turn up as a very central point in charts of several fires and explosions.

Calculating the **Vertex** is reasonably painless, but it does require a **Table of Houses**.

❶ Subtract the Latitude of birth from 90° to find the **Co-Latitude**.
❷ Use the Natal IC as if it were the MC, and calculate the Ascendant using the **Co-Latitude**. The result is the **Vertex**.

Let's take my chart as an example yet again. The Latitude for New Orleans is 29N57′16″. We'll start by finding the **Co-Latitude** by subtracting the Latitude from 90°.

```
       90° 00′ 00 ″ =     89° 59′ 60 ″
    −  29° 57′ 16 ″ =     29° 57′ 16 ″
                          ─────────────
                          60° 02′ 44″ Co-Latitude
```

Next, we use my Natal IC (which is at 13♍10) as the Midheaven, and look up the appropriate tables in the Koch Table of Houses. The two tables we'll be using are 10h 56m 0s (12♍39) and 11h 0m 0s (13♍43).

We need to find the **Sidereal Differential,** and we're going to have to use the Midheaven positions to find it. The total distance between the two Midheavens is 56′ of arc. The distance between the first Midheaven and my Natal IC is 31′ of arc. And when we divide 31 by 56, we get the **SD** of 0.5536. For the **LD**, we take the **Co-Latitude** of 60° 02′ 44″, and see that it falls between 60° and 61° in the table of houses, which in turn gives us an **LD** of 0.0456.

To find the **Vertex**, we simply calculate the Ascendant for these two tables, at the **Co-Latitude.**

SD = 0.5536

Cusp	Table 1	Table 2	Difference	Difference x SD	Adjusted ASC (Vertex)
Ascendant	15♏35	16♏12	37′	20.48	15♏55

LD = 0.0456

Cusp	Table 1 Co-Latitude 1	Table 1 Co-Latitude 2	Difference	Difference x LD	Adjusted Cusp (Copy from Above)	VERTEX
ASC	15♏35	14♏43	62′	0.3	15♏55	15♏52

Calculating the Equatorial Ascendant

The **Equatorial Ascendant** is simply the degree of the zodiac that would be rising if one were born at the Equator. To calculate the **Equatorial Ascendant,** simply calculate the Natal Ascendant using the 0° Latitude figures from the Table of Houses. Since this point is being calculated for an exact Latitude, we only need to interpolate between the two tables (as we did for the Midheaven), using the Natal **SD**. The **Equatorial Ascendant** is sometimes incorrectly referred to as the "East Point."

Notes

Appendix A: Answers to Exercises

Lesson 2: Find the Universal Time and Date of Birth

1. January 9, 1954, 00:28
2. September 24, 1976, 16:00
3. May 16, 1944, 20:30
4. April 18, 1961, 10:02
5. November 11, 1954, 17:53
6. February 19, 1970, 19:42
7. June 3, 1981, 19:55
8. January 1, 1973, 06:45
9. October 19, 1960, 14:45
10. July 22, 1980, 18:30

Lesson 3: Longitude and Latitude Conversions and Calculations

Part 1: Adding and Subtracting

1. 20°57′58″
2. 18°09′32″
3. 12♒53′52″
4. 12♈24′31″
5. 8°18′06″
6. 15°15′54″
7. 10°37′11″
8. 13♑32′52″

Part 2: Conversions

9. 18.6136°
10. 7815″
11. 348.5333′
12. 52.2667′
13. 11.8058°
14. 496.4833′
15. 24°51′44″
16. 19°01′30″

17. 48′37″

18. 2′58″

19. 30′44″

20. 9°13′35″

Lesson 4: Interpolating the Planets

Part 1: Calculate the PT for Each of the Following UTs

1. PT = 0.2792
2. PT = 0.8438
3. PT = 0.7014
4. PT = 0.3486
5. PT = 0.9375

6.

Universal Time (UT) of Birth	August 6, 1972 15:28				
Planet Travel (PT) (UT÷24 hrs)	0.6444				
Planet	**Start**	**End**	**Total Travel**	**Travel x PT**	**Birth Position**
☉	13♌37′23″	14♌34′54″	57.5167	37′07″	14♌14

7.

Universal Time (UT) of Birth	March 14, 1966 21:15				
Planet Travel (PT) (UT÷24 hrs)	0.8854				
Planet	**Start**	**End**	**Total Travel**	**Travel x PT**	**Birth Position**
☽	22♐48′15″	5♑09′04″	12.3469	10°55′55″	3♑44

8.

Universal Time (UT) of Birth	February 5, 1966 10:48				
Planet Travel (PT) (UT÷24 hrs)	0.45				
Planet	**Start**	**End**	**Total Travel**	**Travel x PT**	**Birth Position**
♃	27♌59.8℞	27♌52.2℞	7.6′	3.42′	27♌56 ℞

9.

Universal Time (UT) of Birth	May 6, 1961				
Planet Travel (PT) (UT÷24 hrs)	0.1935 (Month PT = 6th of Month ÷ 31 Days in May)				
Planet	**Start**	**End**	**Total Travel**	**Travel x PT**	**Birth Position**
☊	5♓56.5	6♓39.4	42.9′	8.30′	6♓05

10.

Universal Time (UT) of Birth: July 19, 1972 04:55

Planet Travel (PT) (UT÷24 hrs): 0.2049

Planet	Start	End	Total Travel	Travel x PT	Birth Position
☽	3♏50′45″	15♏43′51″	11.885	2°26′07″	6♏17

11.

Universal Time (UT) of Birth: April 14, 1974 12:37

Planet Travel (PT) (UT÷24 hrs): 0.5257

Planet	Start	End	Total Travel	Travel x PT	Birth Position
☉	23♈40′12″	24♈38′58″	58.7667′	30′54″	24♈11

12.

Universal Time (UT) of Birth: January 26, 1978 21:12

Planet Travel (PT) (UT÷24 hrs): 0.8833

Planet	Start	End	Total Travel	Travel x PT	Birth Position
♂	0♌1.9℞	29♋38.6℞	23.3′	20.58′	29♋41 ℞

Lesson 5: Finding the Sidereal Time of Birth

1. 16:37:42
2. 23:18:40
3. 8:11:35
4. 3:37:44
5. 5:42:33
6. 6:12:56
7. 23:15:04 (Remember to add 12 hours for the Southern Hemisphere)
8. 18:53:22 (Remember to add the Longitude Time Equivalent for Eastern Hemisphere)
9. 7:18:18 (Add Longitude Time Equivalent, and add 12 hours for Southern Hemisphere)
10. 11:03:10 (Add Longitude Time Equivalent, and add 12 hours for Southern Hemisphere)

Lesson 6: Interpolating the Angles and House Cusps

Part 1: Find the SD and LD

1. SD = 0.2042
2. SD = 0.3417
3. SD = 0.5833
4. SD = 0.7458
5. LD = 0.3533
6. LD = 0.7831
7. LD = 0.7257
8. LD = 0.8144

Part 2: Calculate the Remaining House Cusps

SD = 0.4833

Cusp	Table 1	Table 2	Difference	Difference x SD	Adjusted Cusp
Ascendant	28♊04	29♊00	56'	27'	28♊31
2nd	23♋26	24♋21	55'	27'	23♋53
3rd	17♌51	18♌51	60'	29'	18♌20
11th	23♈21	24♈31	70'	34'	23♈55
12th	29♉06	00♊07	61'	29'	29♉35

LD = 0.9544

Cusp	Table 1 Latitude 1	Table 1 Latitude 2	Difference	Difference x LD	Adjusted Cusp (Copy from Above)	ACTUAL HOUSE CUSP
ASC	28♊04	28♊37	33'	31'	**28♊31**	29♊02
2nd	23♋26	23♋50	24'	23'	**23♋53**	24♋16
3rd	17♌51	18♌05	14'	13'	**18♌20**	18♌33
11th	23♈21	23♈48	27'	26'	**23♈55**	24♈21
12th	29♉06	29♉42	36'	34'	**29♉35**	00♊09

© 2004 Kevin B. Burk   www.TheRealAstrology.com

Part 3: Calculate the House Cusps for a Southern Hemisphere Chart

10. Chart Location: Lima, Peru, 12S03, 77W03.
    Sidereal Time of Birth: 5:57:24
    Two Sidereal Times from Tables (for SD): 5h 56m 0s   6h 00m 0s
    Two Closest Latitudes from Table (for LD): 10°   15°

SD = 0.35

Cusp	Table 1	Table 2	Difference	Difference x SD	Adjusted Cusp
Ascendant	28♍59	00♎00	61'	21'	29♍20
2nd	00♏29	01♏28	59'	21'	00♏50
3rd	00♐22	01♐17	55'	19'	00♐41
11th	27♋48	28♋43	55'	19'	28♋07
12th	27♌33	28♌32	59'	21'	27♌54

LD = 0.41

Cusp	Table 1 Latitude 1	Table 1 Latitude 2	Difference	Difference x LD	Adjusted Cusp (Copy from Above)	ACTUAL HOUSE CUSP
ASC	28♍59	29♍01	02'	1'	**29♍20**	29♓21
2nd	00♏29	00♏11	(–)18'	(–)7'	**00♏50**	00♉43
3rd	00♐22	29♏59	(–)23'	(–)9'	**00♐41**	00♊32
11th	27♋48	28♋12	24'	10'	**28♋07**	28♑17
12th	27♌33	27♌55	22'	9'	**27♌54**	28♒03

Did you remember to use the opposite sign for the final house cusps because it's a Southern Hemisphere Chart?

Part 4: Calculate and Draw Natal Charts

11.

Part I: Fill In These Blanks (Look Up Information in Ephemeris and Atlas)

Name	Meryl Streep	Time Zone Correction	EDT (+4:00)
Date and Time of Birth	June 22, 1949 8:05 AM	Longitude Time Equivalent	4:57:29
Location of Birth	Summit, New Jersey, USA	Solar Sidereal Correction	1:59
Latitude & Longitude	40N44'29" 74W21'36"	Midnight Sidereal Time	17:59:23

Part II: Calculate the Constants You Will Need

Universal Time (UT) of Birth	12:05 GMT, June 22, 1949
Sidereal Time of Birth	01:08:53
Planet Travel (PT) (UT÷24 hrs)	0.5035
Sidereal Differential	0.2208
Latitude Differential	0.7413

REMEMBER: Add 12 Hours to the Sidereal Time if Southern Hemisphere Chart!

Part III: Interpolate the Planets

Planet	Start	End	Total Travel	Travel x PT	Birth Position
☉	0♋14'12"	1♋11'27"	57.25'	28'50"	0♋43
☽	8♉16'19"	20♉29'25"	12.2183°	6°09'07"	14♉25
☿	10♊2.7	10♊32.6	29.9'	15.1'	10♊18
♀	17♋48.3	19♋1.6	73.3'	36.9'	18♋25
♂	8♊28.7	9♊10.8	42.1'	21.2'	8♊50
♃	0♒34.7 ℞	0♒29.0 ℞	(−) 5.7'	(−) 2.9'	0♒32 ℞
♄	1♍31.7	1♍36.6	4.9'	2.5'	1♍34
♇	4♐14.7 ℞	4♐11.1 ℞	(−) 3.6'	(−) 1.8'	4♐13 ℞
♅	0♋42.3	0♋45.9	3.6'	1.8'	0♋44
♆	12♎23.8 ℞	12♎23.7	0.1'	0	12♎24 ℞
♇	14♌50.4	14♌51.8	1.4'	0.7'	14♌51
☊	23♈29.5 ℞	23♈26.4 ℞	(−) 3.1'	(−) 1.6'	23♈28 ℞

REMEMBER: If the planet is in Retrograde motion, SUBTRACT the Travel x PT from the Start Position to get the Birth Position!

© 2004 Kevin B. Burk   www.TheRealAstrology.com

Part IV: Interpolate the House Cusps

(Copy the Constants you will need from Page 1)

Sidereal Time of Birth	01:08:53
Sidereal Differential (SD)	0.2208
Latitude Differential (LD)	0.7413

Part IV(a): Calculate the Midheaven

Table 1 MC	Table 2 MC	Difference	Difference x SD	Natal MC
18♈26	19♈30	64'	14'	18♈40

Part IV(b): Calculate the Ascendant and the other House Cusps starting with the ADJUSTED Positions

Cusp	Table 1	Table 2	Difference	Difference x SD	Adjusted Cusp
Ascendant	2♌12	2♌59	47'	10'	2♌22
2nd	27♌26	28♌19	53'	12'	27♌38
3rd	22♍52	23♍51	59'	13'	23♍05
11th	3♊37	4♊30	53'	12'	3♊49
12th	5♋40	6♋27	47'	10'	5♋50

Part IV(c): Calculate the Final House Cusp Positions

Cusp	Table 1 Latitude 1	Table 1 Latitude 2	Difference	Difference x LD	Adjusted Cusp (Copy from Above)	ACTUAL HOUSE CUSP
ASC	2♌12	2♌42	30'	22'	2♌22	2♌44
2nd	27♌26	27♌48	22'	16'	27♌38	27♌54
3rd	22♍52	23♍03	11'	8'	23♍05	23♍13
11th	3♊37	4♊16	39'	29'	3♊49	4♊18
12th	5♋40	6♋19	39'	29'	5♋50	6♋19

REMEMBER: If the signs are moving forward as you increase in Latitude, you ADD the Difference x LD to the Adjusted Cusp to find the Actual House Cusp. If the signs are moving backwards, you SUBTRACT the Difference x LD from the Adjusted Cusp to find the Actual House Cusp.

SOUTHERN HEMISPHERE CHARTS: Use the OPPOSITE SIGN of the Actual House Cusps as your final answer.

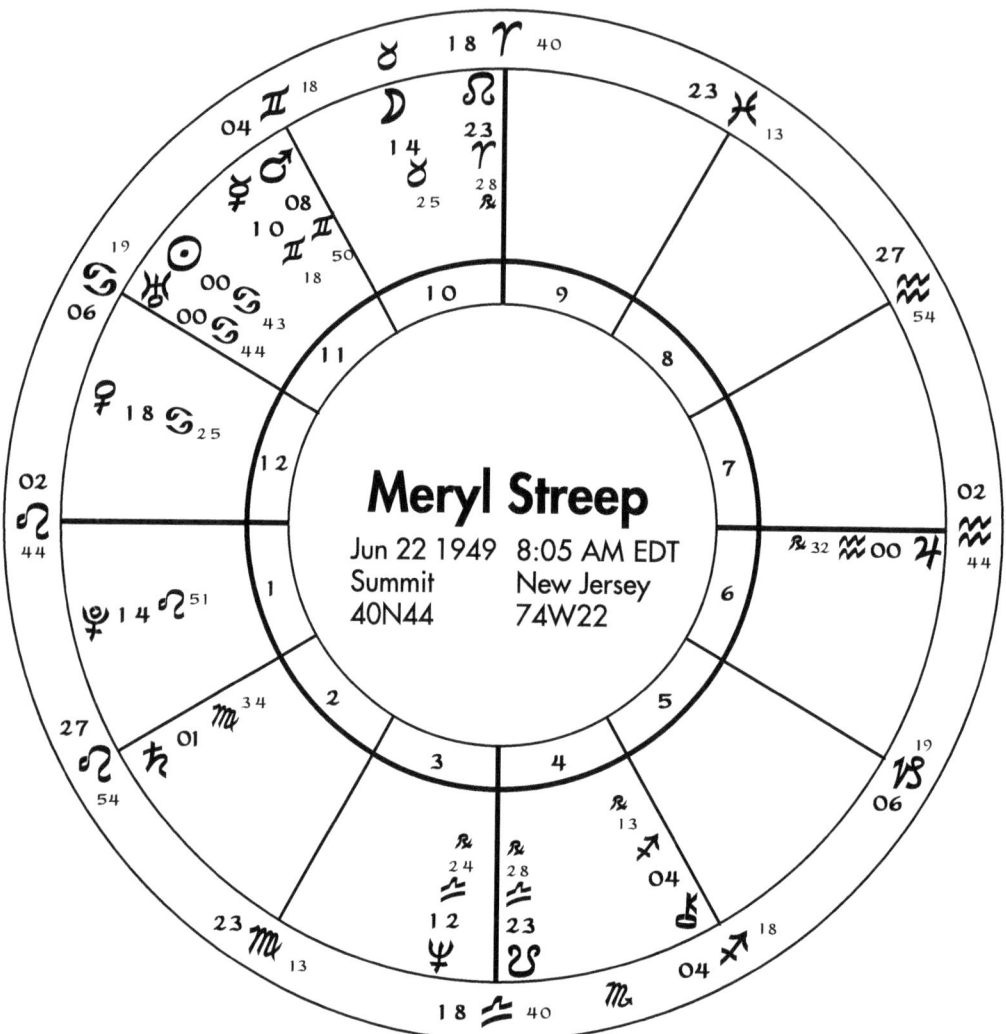

Planet	Position	Angle/Cusp	Position
☉	0♋43	Ascendant (1st)	2♌44
☽	14♉25	2nd House	27♌54
☿	10♊18	3rd House	23♍13
♀	18♋25	4th (IC)	18♎40
♂	8♊50	5th House	4♐18
♃	0♒32 ℞	6th House	6♑19
♄	1♍34	7th (Descendant)	2♒44
⚷	4♐13 ℞	8th House	27♒54
♅	0♋44	9th House	23♓13
♆	12♎24 ℞	Midheaven (10th)	18♈40
♇	14♌51	11th House	4♊18
☊	23♈28 ℞	12th House	6♋19

12.

Part I: Fill In These Blanks (Look Up Information in Ephemeris and Atlas)

Name	Arnold Schwarzenegger	Time Zone Correction	CED (–2:00)
Date and Time of Birth	July 30, 1947 4:10 AM	Longitude Time Equivalent	–1:01:48
Location of Birth	Graz, Austria	Solar Sidereal Correction	0:21
Latitude & Longitude	47N05 15E27	Midnight Sidereal Time	20:27:09

Part II: Calculate the Constants You Will Need

Universal Time (UT) of Birth	02:10 GMT, July 30, 1947
Sidereal Time of Birth	23:39:18
Planet Travel (PT) (UT÷24 hrs)	0.0903
Sidereal Differential	0.825
Latitude Differential	0.0833

REMEMBER: Add 12 Hours to the Sidereal Time if Southern Hemisphere Chart!

Part III: Interpolate the Planets

Planet	Start	End	Total Travel	Travel x PT	Birth Position
☉	6♌00'05"	6♌57'26"	57.35'	5'11"	6♌05"
☽	21♑27'09"	14♑16'35"	11.8239°	1°04'04"	3♑31"
☿	18♋00.3	18♋30.0	29.7'	2.7'	18♋03
♀	26♋15.3	27♋29.1	73.8'	6.7'	26♋22
♂	20♊02.7	20♊43.3	40.6'	3.7'	20♊06
♃	17♏59.4	18♏02.0	2.6'	0.2'	18♏00
♄	11♌34.3	11♌42.0	7.7'	0.7'	11♌35
⚷	3♏00.6	3♏03.7	3.1'	0.3'	3♏01
♅	24♊29.3	24♊32.1	2.8'	0.3'	24♊30
♆	8♎27.1	8♎28.3	1.2'	0.1'	8♎27
♇	12♌45.5	12♌47.3	1.8'	0.2'	12♌46
☊	0♊33.0 ℞	0♊26.0 ℞	7.0'	0.6'	0♊32 ℞

REMEMBER: If the planet is in Retrograde motion, SUBTRACT the Travel x PT from the Start Position to get the Birth Position!

Part IV: Interpolate the House Cusps

(Copy the Constants you will need from Page 1)

Sidereal Time of Birth	23:39:18
Sidereal Differential (SD)	0.825
Latitude Differential (LD)	0.0833

Part IV(a): Calculate the Midheaven

Table 1 MC	Table 2 MC	Difference	Difference x SD	Natal MC
23♓28	24♓33	65'	54'	24♓22

Part IV(b): Calculate the Ascendant and the other House Cusps starting with the ADJUSTED Positions

Cusp	Table 1	Table 2	Difference	Difference x SD	Adjusted Cusp
Ascendant	18♋24	19♋11	47'	39'	19♋03
2nd	10♌31	11♌22	51'	42'	11♌13
3rd	1♍56	2♍54	58'	48'	2♍44
11th	17♉33	18♉36	63'	52'	18♉25
12th	23♊00	23♊50	50'	41'	23♊41

Part IV(c): Calculate the Final House Cusp Positions

Cusp	Table 1 Latitude 1	Table 1 Latitude 2	Difference	Difference x LD	Adjusted Cusp (Copy from Above)	ACTUAL HOUSE CUSP
ASC	18♋24	19♋11	47'	4'	**19♋03**	19♋07
2nd	10♌31	11♌02	31'	3'	**11♌13**	11♌16
3rd	1♍56	2♍12	16'	1'	**2♍44**	2♍45
11th	17♉33	18♉46	73'	6'	**18♉25**	18♉31
12th	23♊00	24♊05	65'	5'	**23♊41**	23♊46

REMEMBER: If the signs are moving forward as you increase in Latitude, you ADD the Difference x LD to the Adjusted Cusp to find the Actual House Cusp. If the signs are moving backwards, you SUBTRACT the Difference x LD from the Adjusted Cusp to find the Actual House Cusp.

SOUTHERN HEMISPHERE CHARTS: Use the OPPOSITE SIGN of the Actual House Cusps as your final answer.

© 2004 Kevin B. Burk   www.TheRealAstrology.com

APPENDIX A: ANSWERS TO EXERCISES PAGE A-11

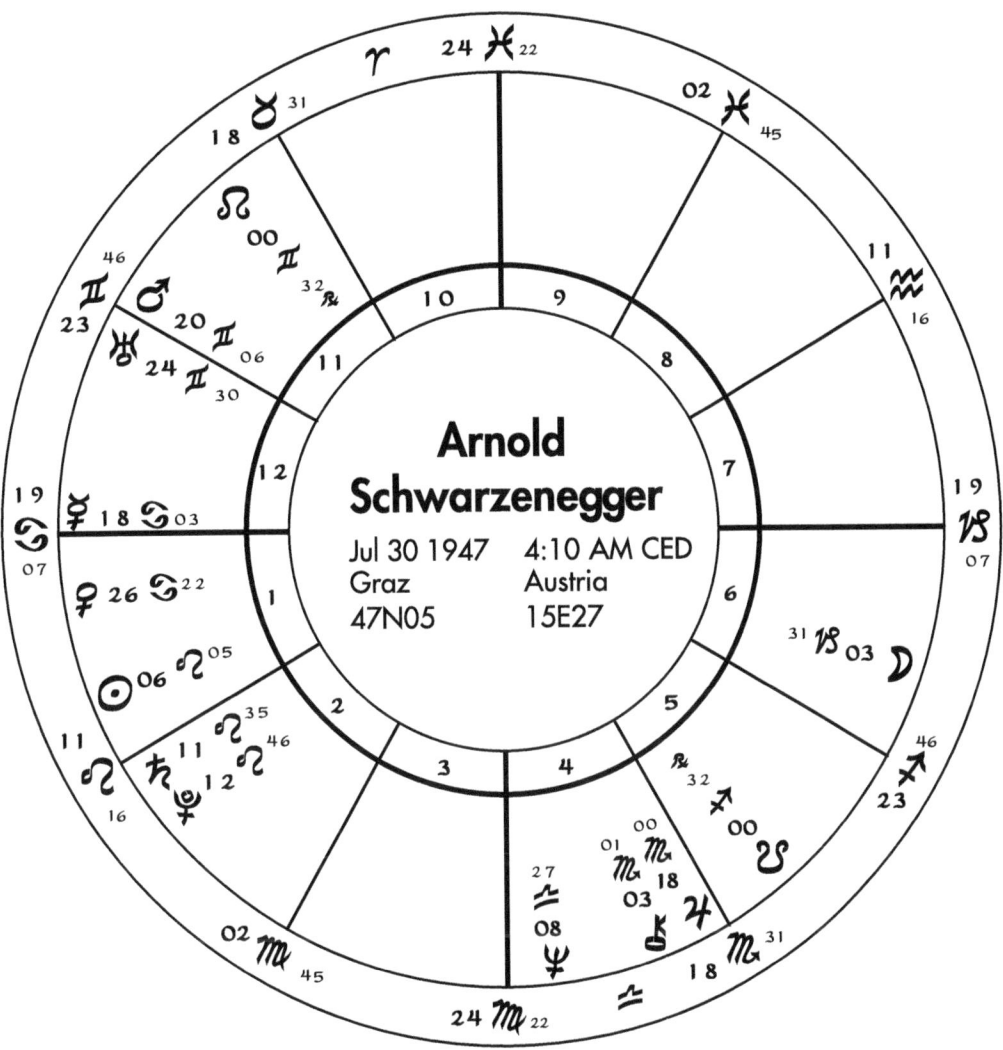

Planet	Position	Angle/Cusp	Position
☉	6♌05″	Ascendant (1st)	19♋07
☽	3♑31″	2nd House	11♌16
☿	18♋03	3rd House	2♍45
♀	26♋22	4th (IC)	24♍22
♂	20♊06	5th House	18♏31
♃	18♏00	6th House	23♐46
♄	11♌35	7th (Descendant)	19♑07
⚷	3♏01	8th House	11♒16
♅	24♊30	9th House	2♓45
♆	8♎27	Midheaven (10th)	24♓22
♇	12♌46	11th House	18♉31
☊	0♊32 ℞	12th House	23♊46

www.TheRealAstrology.com ©2004 Kevin B. Burk

13.

Part I: Fill In These Blanks (Look Up Information in Ephemeris and Atlas)

Name	Evita Peron	Time Zone Correction	AROT (4:17)
Date and Time of Birth	May 7, 1919 5:00 AM	Longitude Time Equivalent	3:53:48
Location of Birth	Buenos Aires, Argentina	Solar Sidereal Correction	1:32
Latitude & Longitude	34S36 58W27	Midnight Sidereal Time	14:55:09

Part II: Calculate the Constants You Will Need

Universal Time (UT) of Birth	09:17 GMT May 7, 1919
Sidereal Time of Birth	8:19:53
Planet Travel (PT) (UT÷24 hrs)	0.387
Sidereal Differential	0.971
Latitude Differential	0.6

REMEMBER: Add 12 Hours to the Sidereal Time if Southern Hemisphere Chart!

Part III: Interpolate the Planets

Planet	Start	End	Total Travel	Travel x PT	Birth Position
☉	15♉23'18"	16♉21'22"	58.07'	22'28"	15♉56
☽	15♌36'37"	28♌25'01"	12.807°	4°57'23"	20♌34
☿	18♈57.9	19♈59.9	62.0'	23.9'	19♈22
♀	23♊16.6	24♊26.5	69.9'	27.0'	23♊44
♂	16♉3.2	16♉46.8	43.6'	16.8'	16♉20
♃	11♋51.5	12♋1.6	10.1'	3.9'	11♋55
♄	21♌30.3	21♌31.8	1.5'	0.6'	21♌31
♇	5♈17.6	5♈20.5	2.9'	1.1'	5♈19
♅	1♓19.1	1♓20.5	1.4'	0.6'	1♓20
♆	6♌37.5	6♌38.2	0.7'	0.3'	6♌38
♇	4♋58.9	4♋59.9	1.0'	0.4'	4♋59
☊	04♐0.3 ℞	03♐59.9 ℞	(−) 0.4'	(−) 0.1'	04♐00 ℞

REMEMBER: If the planet is in Retrograde motion, SUBTRACT the Travel x PT from the Start Position to get the Birth Position!

Part IV: Interpolate the House Cusps

(Copy the Constants you will need from Page 1)

Sidereal Time of Birth	8:19:53
Sidereal Differential (SD)	0.971
Latitude Differential (LD)	0.6

Part IV(a): Calculate the Midheaven

Table 1 MC	Table 2 MC	Difference	Difference x SD	Natal MC
1♌45	2♌43	58'	56'	2♒41

Part IV(b): Calculate the Ascendant and the other House Cusps starting with the ADJUSTED Positions

Cusp	Table 1	Table 2	Difference	Difference x SD	Adjusted Cusp
Ascendant	28♎31	29♎21	50'	48.6'	29♎20
2nd	27♏08	27♏55	47'	45.6'	27♏54
3rd	26♐41	27♐29	48'	46.6'	27♐28
11th	00♍21	01♍17	56'	54.4'	01♍15
12th	29♍26	00♎19	53'	51.5'	00♎17

Part IV(c): Calculate the Final House Cusp Positions

Cusp	Table 1 Latitude 1	Table 1 Latitude 2	Difference	Difference x LD	Adjusted Cusp (Copy from Above)	ACTUAL HOUSE CUSP
ASC	28♎31	28♎17	(−) 14'	(−) 8.4'	29♎20	29♈12
2nd	27♏08	26♏50	(−) 18'	(−) 10.8'	27♏54	27♉43
3rd	26♐41	26♐24	(−) 17'	(−) 10.2'	27♐28	27♊18
11th	00♍21	00♍18	(−) 3'	(−) 1.8'	01♍15	01♓13
12th	29♍26	29♍17	(−) 9'	(−) 5.4'	00♎17	00♈12

REMEMBER: If the signs are moving forward as you increase in Latitude, you ADD the Difference x LD to the Adjusted Cusp to find the Actual House Cusp. If the signs are moving backwards, you SUBTRACT the Difference x LD from the Adjusted Cusp to find the Actual House Cusp.

SOUTHERN HEMISPHERE CHARTS: Use the OPPOSITE SIGN of the Actual House Cusps as your final answer.

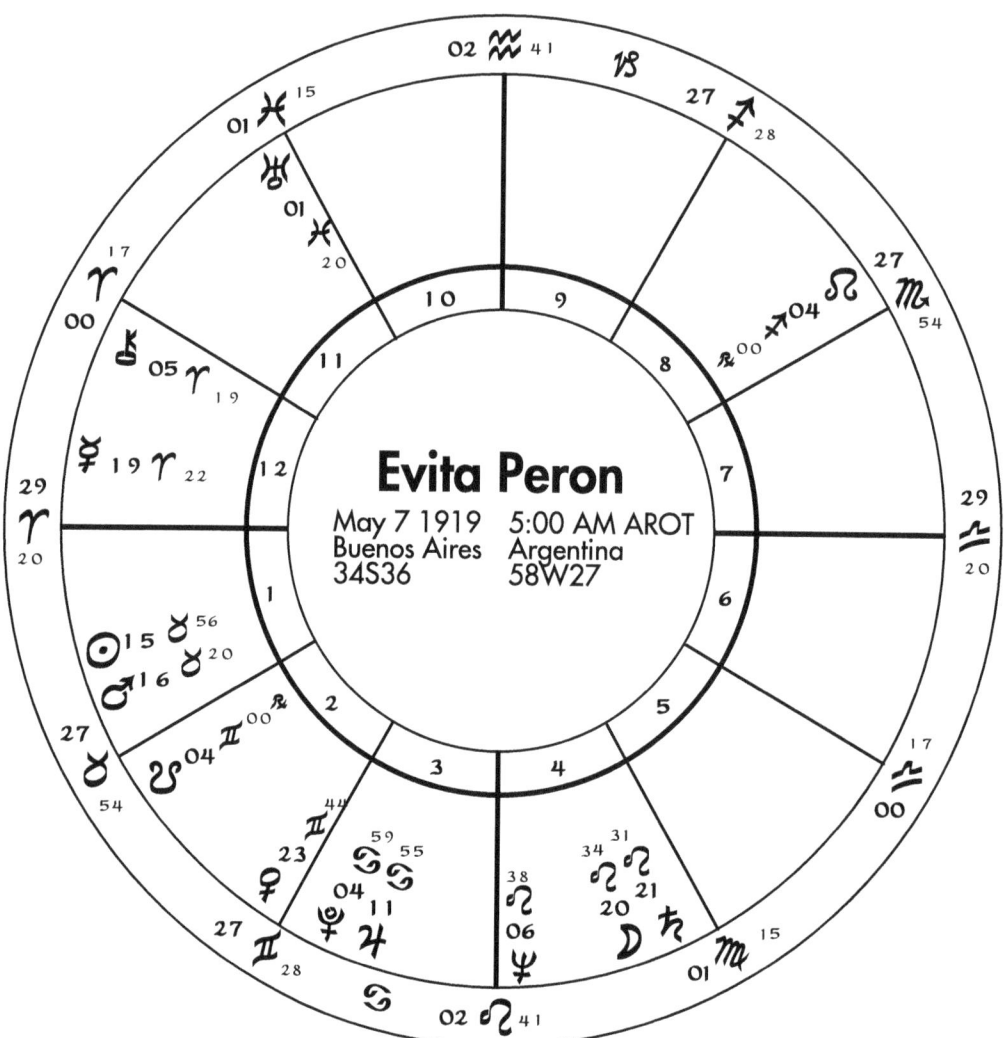

Planet	Position	Angle/Cusp	Position
☉	15♉56	Ascendant (1st)	29♈20
☽	20♌34	2nd House	27♉54
☿	19♈22	3rd House	27♊28
♀	23♊44	4th (IC)	02♌41
♂	16♉20	5th House	01♍15
♃	11♋55	6th House	00♎17
♄	21♌31	7th (Descendant)	29♎20
⚷	5♈19	8th House	27♏ ♋
♅	1♓20	9th House	27♐28
♆	6♌38	Midheaven (10th)	02♒41
♇	4♋59	11th House	01♓15
☊	04♐00 ℞	12th House	00♈17

14.

Part I: Fill In These Blanks (Look Up Information in Ephemeris and Atlas)

Name	Rupert Murdoch	Time Zone Correction	AEST (–10:00)
Date and Time of Birth	March 11, 1931 11:59 PM	Longitude Time Equivalent	–9:39:52
Location of Birth	Melbourne, Australia	Solar Sidereal Correction	2:18
Latitude & Longitude	37S49 144E58	Midnight Sidereal Time	11:10:46

Part II: Calculate the Constants You Will Need

Universal Time (UT) of Birth	13:59 GMT, March 11, 1931
Sidereal Time of Birth	22:51:56
Planet Travel (PT) (UT÷24 hrs)	0.5826
Sidereal Differential	0.9833
Latitude Differential	0.8167

REMEMBER: Add 12 Hours to the Sidereal Time if Southern Hemisphere Chart!

Part III: Interpolate the Planets

Planet	Start	End	Total Travel	Travel x PT	Birth Position
☉	19♓27'18"	20♓27'12"	59.9'	34'54"	20♓02
☽	16♐50'19"	29♐39'32"	12.8203°	7°28'09"	24♐18
☿	14♓51.3	16♓44.1	112.8'	65.7'	15♓57
♀	5♒49.0	6♒57.9	68.9'	40.1'	06♒29
♂	27♋27.9	27♋30.0	2.1'	1.2'	27♋29
♃	10♋28.2	10♋29.1	0.9'	0.5'	10♋29
♄	21♑02.1	21♑06.9	4.8'	2.8'	21♑05
⚷	15♉04.2	15♉06.9	2.7'	1.6'	15♉06
♅	13♈52.3	13♈55.5	3.2'	1.9'	13♈54
♆	3♍59.9 ℞	3♍58.3 ℞	(–) 1.6'	(–) 0.9'	3♍59 ℞
♇	18♋47.5 ℞	18♋46.9 ℞	(–) 0.6'	(–) 0.3'	18♋47 ℞
☊	14♈40.2 ℞	14♈39.9 ℞	(–) 0.3'	(–) 0.2'	14♈40 ℞

REMEMBER: If the planet is in Retrograde motion, SUBTRACT the Travel x PT from the Start Position to get the Birth Position!

Part IV: Interpolate the House Cusps

(Copy the Constants you will need from Page 1)

Sidereal Time of Birth	22:51:56
Sidereal Differential (SD)	0.9833
Latitude Differential (LD)	0.8167

Part IV(a): Calculate the Midheaven

Table 1 MC	Table 2 MC	Difference	Difference x SD	Natal MC
10♓30	11♓34	64'	63'	11♍33

Part IV(b): Calculate the Ascendant and the other House Cusps starting with the ADJUSTED Positions

Cusp	Table 1	Table 2	Difference	Difference x SD	Adjusted Cusp
Ascendant	00♋59	01♋54	55'	54.1'	01♋53
2nd	25♋31	25♋57	26'	25.6'	25♋57
3rd	18♌01	18♌44	43'	42.3'	18♌43
11th	25♈08	26♈20	72'	70.8'	26♈19
12th	02♊31	03♊32	61'	60.0'	03♊31

Part IV(c): Calculate the Final House Cusp Positions

Cusp	Table 1 Latitude 1	Table 1 Latitude 2	Difference	Difference x LD	Adjusted Cusp (Copy from Above)	ACTUAL HOUSE CUSP
ASC	00♋59	01♋39	40'	32.7'	01♋53	02♑26
2nd	25♋31	26♋00	29'	23.7'	25♋57	26♑21
3rd	18♌01	18♌16	15'	12.3'	18♌43	18♒55
11th	25♈08	25♈47	39'	31.9'	26♈19	26♎51
12th	02♊31	03♊19	48'	39.2'	03♊31	04♐10

REMEMBER: If the signs are moving forward as you increase in Latitude, you ADD the Difference x LD to the Adjusted Cusp to find the Actual House Cusp. If the signs are moving backwards, you SUBTRACT the Difference x LD from the Adjusted Cusp to find the Actual House Cusp.

SOUTHERN HEMISPHERE CHARTS: Use the OPPOSITE SIGN of the Actual House Cusps as your final answer.

Appendix A: Answers to Exercises

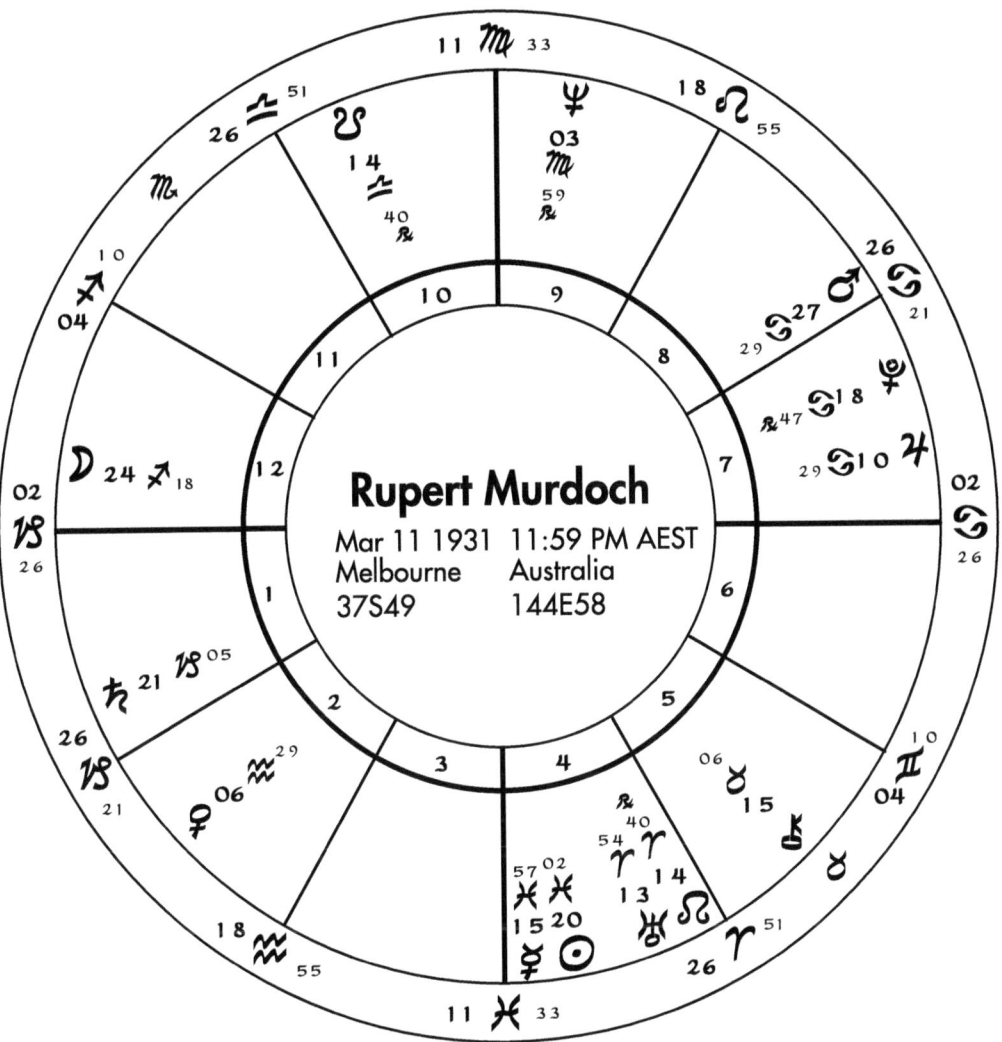

Planet	Position	Angle/Cusp	Position
☉	20♓02	Ascendant (1st)	02♑26
☽	24♐18	2nd House	26♑21
☿	15♓57	3rd House	18♒55
♀	06♒29	4th (IC)	11♓33
♂	27♋29	5th House	26♈51
♃	10♋29	6th House	04♊10
♄	21♑05	7th (Descendant)	02♋26
♆	15♉06	8th House	26♋21
♅	13♈54	9th House	18♌55
♆	3♍59 ℞	Midheaven (10th)	11♍33
♇	18♋47 ℞	11th House	26♎51
☊	14♈40 ℞	12th House	04♐10

Lesson 7: Relocated Charts

Name	Relocated To:	Answer:
Meryl Streep	Honolulu	M
	Jakarta	B
	Los Angeles	O
	Paris	D
Arnold Schwarzenegger	Honolulu	E
	Jakarta	K
	Los Angeles	H
	Paris	P
Evita Peron	Honolulu	F
	Jakarta	L
	Los Angeles	I
	Paris	A
Rupert Murdoch	Honolulu	G
	Jakarta	N
	Los Angeles	J
	Paris	C

	Sidereal Tables
A	0h 20m 0s – 0h 24m 0s
B	1h 12m 0s – 1h 16m 0s
C	1h 20m 0s – 1h 24m 0s
D	6h 12m 0s – 6h 16m 0s
E	12h 04m 0s – 12h 08m 0s
F	13h 40m 0s – 13h 44m 0s
G	14h 40m 0s – 14h 44m 0s
H	14h 44m 0s – 14h 48m 0s
I	16h 20m 0s – 16h 24m 0s
J	17h 16m 0s – 17h 20m 0s
K	17h 44m 0s – 17h 48m 0s
L	19h 20m 0s – 19h 24m 0s
M	19h 32m 0s – 19h 36m 0s
N	20h 16m 0s – 20h 20m 0s
O	22h 12m 0s – 22h 16m 0s
P	22h 44m 0s – 22h 48m 0s

Lesson 8: Find the UT of the Return Charts

	Natal Position	Date 1 Position	Date 2 Position	PT	UT of Return
1.	16♐21'13"	15♐25'56"	16♐26'53"	0.9070	21:46:05
2.	4♓59'46"	28♒25'41"	11♓49'08"	0.4905	11:46:19
3.	29♊40'24"	19♊14'38"	4♋32'19"	0.6819	16:21:56
4.	12♈10'52"	11♈34'03"	12♈33'16"	0.6217	14:55:15
5.	3♒02'11"	2♒16'21"	3♒17'22"	0.7512	18:01:44

Lesson 9: Calculate the PPT

	Progress-To-Date	ACD	Difference	PPT
1.	May 23, 1995	March 18	66	0.1808
2.	September 6, 1980	July 4	65	0.1776
3.	March 5, 1997	October 25	131	0.3589
4.	November 29, 1973	April 18	225	0.6164
5.	February 1, 1992	December 6	57	0.1562

NOTE: Make sure that you adjust for Leap Years when aplicable. In example number 2, Sepbember 6, 1980 is day **250**, and we divide the difference in days by 366 because of the leap year.

Notes

Appendix B: Astrology Math Formulas

Converting From Standard Clock Time to Military Time

To convert from a standard 12-hour (A.M./P.M.) clock time to **Military Time** (24-hour clock) add 12 hours if the time is P.M., and drop the A.M./P.M. designation. **Military Time** runs from 00:00 (midnight) to 23:59 (11:59 P.M.).

Calculating the UT of Birth

For Birth Locations West of Greenwich

1. Convert the local time of birth into **Military Time** (24 hour clock)
2. Add the **Time Zone Offset** (found in the **Atlas**)
3. If the result is greater than 24 hours, subtract 24 hours from the total and add one day to the date of birth.

For Birth Locations East of Greenwich

1. Convert the local time of birth into **Military Time** (24 hour clock)
2. Subtract the **Time Zone Offset** (found in the **Atlas**)
3. If the result is less than zero hours, add 24 hours to the total and subtract one day from the date of birth.

Calculating the Planet Travel (PT) Constant to Interpolate Planets

1. Convert the UT of birth into terms of hours.
2. Divide the UT by 24 hours in a day to find the PT constant.

Calculating the Sidereal Time of Birth

Sidereal Time for the Northern and Western Hemispheres

Universal Time of Birth
+ Solar-Sidereal Correction (SSC)
+ Midnight Sidereal Time from Ephemeris for UT of Birth
− Longitude Time Equivalent (From Atlas)
───────────────────────────────
Sidereal Time of Birth

Remember to adjust the final answer so that it fits within the range of 0–24 hours.

Sidereal Time for the Northern and Eastern Hemispheres

	Universal Time of Birth
+	Solar-Sidereal Correction (SSC)
+	Midnight Sidereal Time from Ephemeris for UT of Birth
+	Longitude Time Equivalent (From Atlas)
	Sidereal Time of Birth

Remember to adjust the final answer so that it fits within the range of 0–24 hours. For locations in the Eastern Hemisphere, you will add the **Longitude Time Equivalent** from the atlas.

Sidereal Time for the Southern and Western Hemispheres

	Universal Time of Birth
+	Solar-Sidereal Correction (SSC)
+	Midnight Sidereal Time from Ephemeris for UT of Birth
−	Longitude Time Equivalent (From Atlas)
+	12 Hours to Adjust for Southern Hemisphere (offset later by reversing the cusps)
	Sidereal Time of Birth, fudged to allow the use of a Northern Hemisphere House Table

Remember to adjust the final answer so that it fits within the range of 0–24 hours.

Sidereal Time for the Southern and Eastern Hemispheres

	Universal Time of Birth
+	Solar-Sidereal Correction (SSC)
+	Midnight Sidereal Time from Ephemeris for UT of Birth
+	Longitude Time Equivalent (From Atlas)
+	12 Hours to Adjust for Southern Hemisphere (offset later by reversing the cusps)
	Sidereal Time of Birth, fudged to allow the use of a Northern Hemisphere House Table

Remember to adjust the final answer so that it fits within the range of 0–24 hours. For locations in the Eastern Hemisphere, you will add the **Longitude Time Equivalent** from the atlas.

Calculating the Sidereal Time for Relocated Charts

Sidereal Time for Relocations in the Northern and Western Hemispheres

      Universal Time of Birth
+   Solar-Sidereal Correction (SSC)
+   Midnight Sidereal Time from Ephemeris for UT of Birth
−   Longitude Time Equivalent *for Relocated Destination* (From Atlas)
_____
      Relocated Sidereal Time

Remember to adjust the final answer so that it fits within the range of 0–24 hours.

Sidereal Time for Relocations in the Northern and Eastern Hemispheres

      Universal Time of Birth
+   Solar-Sidereal Correction (SSC)
+   Midnight Sidereal Time from Ephemeris for UT of Birth
+   Longitude Time Equivalent *for Relocated Destination* (From Atlas)
_____
      Relocated Sidereal Time

Remember to adjust the final answer so that it fits within the range of 0–24 hours. For locations in the Eastern Hemisphere, you will **add** the **Longitude Time Equivalent** from the atlas.

Sidereal Time for Relocations in the Southern and Western Hemispheres

      Universal Time of Birth
+   Solar-Sidereal Correction (SSC)
+   Midnight Sidereal Time from Ephemeris for UT of Birth
−   Longitude Time Equivalent *for Relocated Destination* (From Atlas)
+   12 Hours to Adjust for Southern Hemisphere (offset later by reversing the cusps)
_____
      Relocated Sidereal Time, fudged to allow the use of a Northern Hemisphere House Table

Remember to adjust the final answer so that it fits within the range of 0–24 hours.

Sidereal Time for Relocations in the Southern and Eastern Hemispheres

      Universal Time of Birth
+   Solar-Sidereal Correction (SSC)
+   Midnight Sidereal Time from Ephemeris for UT of Birth
+   Longitude Time Equivalent *for Relocated Destination* (From Atlas)
+   12 Hours to Adjust for Southern Hemisphere (offset later by reversing the cusps)
_____
      Relocated Sidereal Time, fudged to allow for use of a Northern Hemisphere House Table

Remember to adjust the final answer so that it fits within the range of 0–24 hours. For locations in the Eastern Hemisphere, you will **add** the **Longitude Time Equivalent** from the atlas.

Calculating the Progressed Planet Travel (PPT) Constant

❶ Convert both the ACD and the **Progress-to-Date** into **Julian Days** (1–365, or 1–366 in a leap year)

❷ Subtract the ACD from the **Progress-to-Date** to find the difference between them.

$$\begin{array}{r} \text{Progress-to-Date (Julian)} \\ - \text{ACD (Julian)} \\ \hline \text{Difference} \end{array}$$

❸ Divide this difference by the total number of days in the year to find the **PPT** constant. Use 365 days unless there is a February 29th between the ACD that precedes the **Progress-to-Date**, and the ACD following. In the latter case, use 366 days.

Finding the Adjusted Calculation Date for Secondary Progressions

$$\begin{array}{r} \text{Midnight Sidereal Time from Ephemeris for UT of Birth} \\ - \text{UT of Birth} \\ \hline \text{ACD Sidereal Time} \end{array}$$

Look up the ACD **Sidereal Time** in the ephemeris. The ACD is the date with the listed **Midnight Sidereal Time** closest to the ACD **Sidereal Time**.

Calculating Precession for Return Charts

$$\begin{array}{r} \text{Natal Synetic Vernal Point (SVP) from Ephemeris} \\ - \text{Return Date Synetic Vernal Point (SVP) from Ephemeris} \\ \hline \text{Precession} \end{array}$$

Calculating the Vertex

❶ Subtract the Latitude of birth from 90° to find the **Co-Latitude**.

❷ Use the Natal IC as if it were the MC, and calculate the Ascendant using the **Co-Latitude**. The result is the **Vertex**.

Calculating the Equatorial Ascendant

Calculate the Natal Ascendant using the 0° Latitude figures from the Table of Houses.

Appendix C: Natal Chart Calculation Worksheet

The following pages contain a blank **Natal Chart Calculation Worksheet**. Use this form to practice calculating natal charts on your own.

You can download a PDF of this worksheet so you can print additional copies. Visit www.TheRealAstrology.com/MATH/.

Part I: Fill In These Blanks (Look Up Information in Ephemeris and Atlas)

Name _____

Date and Time of Birth _____

Location of Birth _____

Latitude & Longitude _____

Time Zone Correction _____

Longitude Time Equivalent _____

Solar Sidereal Correction _____

Midnight Sidereal Time _____

Part II: Calculate the Constants You Will Need

Universal Time (UT) of Birth _____

Sidereal Time of Birth _____

Planet Travel (PT) (UT÷24 hrs) _____

Sidereal Differential _____

Latitude Differential _____

REMEMBER: Add 12 Hours to the Sidereal Time if Southern Hemisphere Chart!

Part III: Interpolate the Planets

Planet	Start	End	Total Travel	Travel x PT	Birth Position
☉					
☽					
☿					
♀					
♂					
♃					
♄					
⚷					
♅					
♆					
♇					
☊					

REMEMBER: If the planet is in Retrograde motion, SUBTRACT the Travel x PT from the Start Position to get the Birth Position!

© 2004 Kevin B. Burk   www.TheRealAstrology.com

Part IV: Interpolate the House Cusps

(Copy the Constants you will need from Page 1)

Sidereal Time of Birth _____

Sidereal Differential (SD) _____

Latitude Differential (LD) _____

Part IV(a): Calculate the Midheaven

Table 1 MC	Table 2 MC	Difference	Difference x SD	Natal MC

Part IV(b): Calculate the Ascendant and the other House Cusps starting with the ADJUSTED Positions

Cusp	Table 1	Table 2	Difference	Difference x SD	Adjusted Cusp
Ascendant					
2nd					
3rd					
11th					
12th					

Part IV(c): Calculate the Final House Cusp Positions

Cusp	Table 1 Latitude 1	Table 1 Latitude 2	Difference	Difference x LD	Adjusted Cusp (Copy from Above)	ACTUAL HOUSE CUSP
ASC						
2nd						
3rd						
11th						
12th						

REMEMBER: If the signs are moving forward as you increase in Latitude, you ADD the Difference x LD to the Adjusted Cusp to find the Actual House Cusp. If the signs are moving backwards, you SUBTRACT the Difference x LD from the Adjusted Cusp to find the Actual House Cusp.

SOUTHERN HEMISPHERE CHARTS: Use the OPPOSITE SIGN of the Actual House Cusps as your final answer.

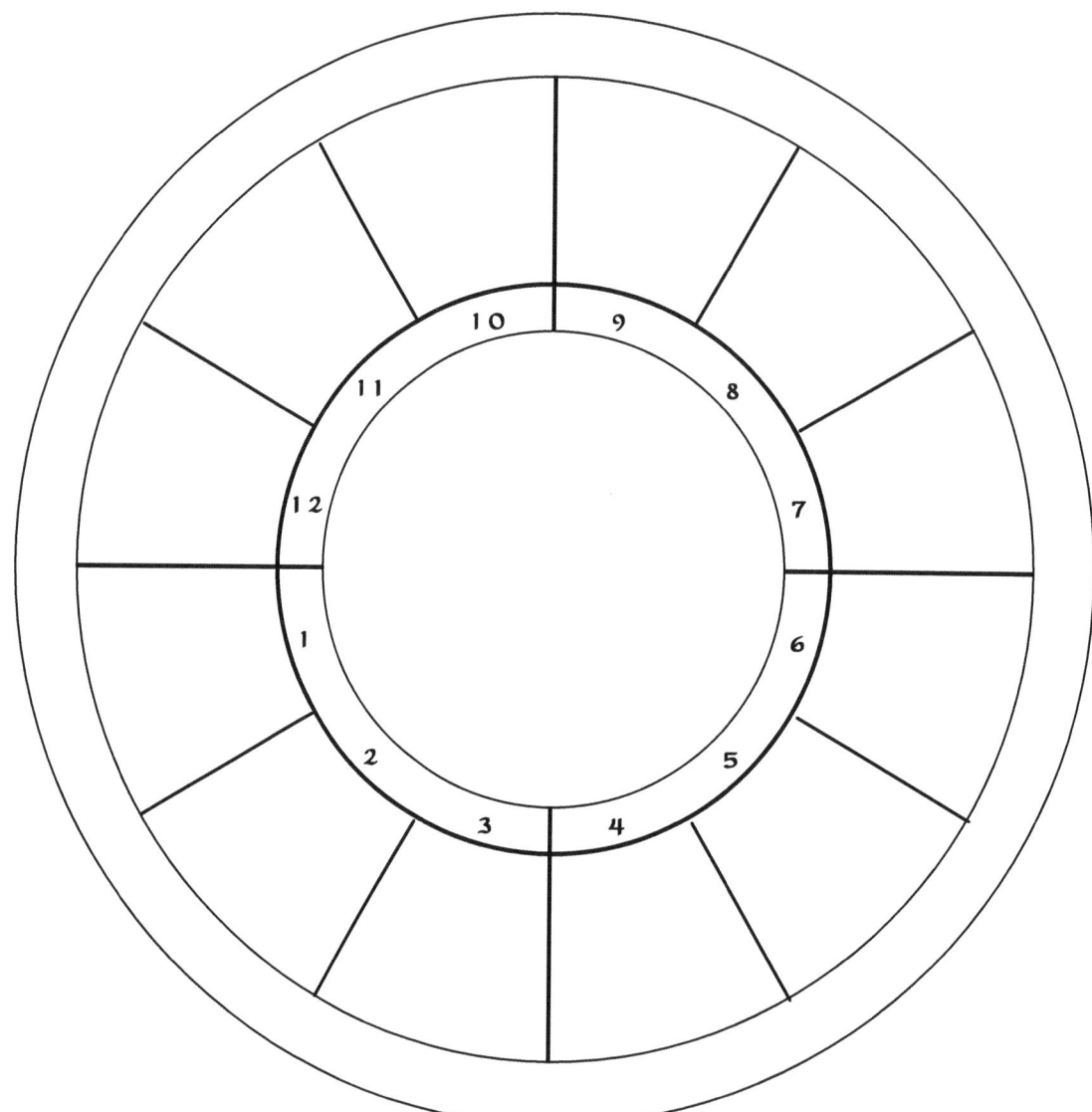

Planet	Position	Angle/Cusp	Position
☉		Ascendant (1st)	
☽		2nd House	
☿		3rd House	
♀		4th (IC)	
♂		5th House	
♃		6th House	
♄		7th (Descendant)	
⚷		8th House	
♅		9th House	
♆		Midheaven (10th)	
♇		11th House	
☊		12th House	

A COMPLETE REFERENCE LIBRARY AT AN INCREDIBLE SAVINGS!

Whether you are planning to attend astrology classes or complete your certification, ACS reference books are an absolute necessity for hand-calculating charts. With Astro's high standards of accuracy, these reference materials are an indispensable part of every astrologer's library. **The Reference Book Package** provides you with all the essential texts at a fraction of the regular cost. Includes:

- American Ephemeris for the 21st Century - Midnight Hardcover (Reg. $29.95)
- American Ephemeris for the 20th Century - Midnight (Reg. $21.95)
- American Atlas (Reg. $39.95) • International Atlas (Reg. $39.95)
- Michelsen Book of Tables (Reg. $15.95)

A $147.75 value for only $99.95! (+s/h)

You will also receive, ABSOLUTELY FREE, a package of 25 blank chart wheels.

THE ANCIENT ART OF ASTROLOGY MEETS THE POWER OF YOUR COMPUTER!

ACS Publications, the company that sets the standards for accuracy in astrological calculations, is proud to present the **Electronic Astrologer Series**—three Windows programs that offer the most comprehensive information and highest level of accuracy in calculating and interpreting birth charts, future trends, and romantic compatibility—now at an incredible savings!

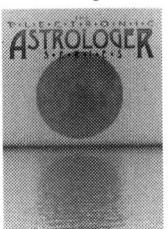

- **No prior knowledge of astrology required** - all information presented in an easy-to-understand format.
- **Easy to use** - all you need is the date, time and place of birth for each person; ability to store hundreds of charts. Covers a 200-year period from 1850 to 2050.
- **Color-Coded Horoscope Wheels, Keyword Search and Dynamic Cursor** to guide you through your horoscope with minimal effort and maximum results.
- **Unparalleled HELP System** - with extensive data on all aspects of chart interpretation and enough information for a complete encyclopedia of astrology.
- **Built-in Atlas** - extensive database of over 9,000 cities and hospitals worldwide with longitude, latitude and time change information (daylight, standard, war time).

The Electronic Astrologer Reveals Your Horoscope
Learn about your inner drives, talents, behavior patterns, stresses and challenges. This complete birth chart with interpretation includes a 40-50 page report detailing planets in signs, planets in houses, planet to planet aspects, signs on house cusp, placement of house rulers by house and sign. Voted the "Best Beginner's Program" by American Astrology Magazine.

The Electronic Astrologer Reveals Your Future
Full of insights and suggestions to make the most of any aspect, this program will help you to see the future of your love life, spirituality, career, travel and more. Incorporating the two most popular methods of forecasting, the EA Future offers a comprehensive look ahead using secondary progressions and transits. Voted "Best Program of the Year" by American Astrology Magazine.

The Electronic Astrologer Reveals Your Romance
Is he your soulmate? Is she the right one for you? This program features a two-wheel chart to easily spot the "connections" between partners, a relationship grid which calculates scores for attraction, affection, togetherness, sexual sizzle and an overall "Love Line," and a comprehensive report detailing how each couple handles issues of communication, love, assertion, sex, home and family.

System Requirements:
Windows '95 or higher with a CD-ROM Drive; 12MB of free hard disk space; Pentium or higher processor.

Order IBMWEA3 .... **$175.00**   (Individual programs are available at $69.95 each.)

Astro Communications Services, Inc.
(800) 514-8070 • www.AstroCom.com
When it comes to Astrology, we wrote the book!

by Kevin B. Burk

The first truly comprehensive guide to human relationships has finally arrived! *The Relationship Handbook* is guaranteed to help you to improve *every single relationship* in your life! Inside, you will learn the secrets to improving your romantic relationships, your family relationships, your professional relationships, and even your friendships!

Filled with practical, compassionate, often humorous but always useful advice, *The Relationship Handbook* guides you through the ins and outs of all human relationships.

The Relationship Handbook changes people's lives. In the words of one of the many participants of Kevin B. Burk's Relationship Workshops, **"This information makes my world a better place to live!"**

In The Relationship Handbook you will discover...

❖ The two most important needs in every relationship—*and why we're almost never aware of one of them!*
❖ How to move from fear into love and master our spiritual lessons.
❖ The three elements that define *every* romantic relationship.
❖ The blueprints that determine how you create every one of your relationships.
❖ How to overcome your negative thinking and create the loving, supportive relationships that you deserve.
❖ The *real* differences between men and women (and it's got nothing to do with being from different planets)!
❖ The Relationship Definition Talk—the key to successful romantic relationships.
❖ Six steps that are guaranteed to improve *every* relationship in your life.
❖ ...and much more!

THE RELATIONSHIP HANDBOOK *by* **KEVIN B. BURK**
SERENDIPITY PRESS, OCTOBER 2004
HARDBACK/ISBN 0-9759682-1-1/$29.95 U.S.
619.807.2473 • 6161 EL CAJON BLVD #306, SAN DIEGO CA • WWW.EVERYRELATIONSHIP.COM
CONTACT: KEVIN BURK, 619.807.2473 • KEVIN@EVERYRELATIONSHIP.COM

by Kevin B. Burk

When most people begin to study astrology, the first thing they want to know is what their birth chart has to say about them. The second thing they want to know is what their birth chart has to say about their relationships.

This is hardly surprising. Relationships are the most important aspects of our lives. From the moment we arrive on Earth to the moment we depart, we experience relationships of all kinds with other individuals. Sometimes these relationships are supportive, and sometimes they present challenges. Some people have a knack for maintaining strong and healthy relationships. The rest of us, however, wish we had some help.

That help has finally arrived!

In this handbook, you will learn everything you need to use astrology to understand and improve your relationships. You will learn how to use classical astrology to create a context for understanding each individual birth chart. And you will learn how to build on this foundation and discover how to compare two natal charts and identify the key challenges and opportunities in any relationship.

The Astrological Relationship Handbook will reveal...

- ❖ How to use the birth chart to **unlock the secrets** of exactly what you need in every one of your relationships.
- ❖ Why the Sun has **nothing to do with compatibility** (and which planets you should be considering!).
- ❖ The **only way to evaluate compatibility** in relationships by considering two individuals and not two charts.
- ❖ ...and much, much more!

ASTROLOGICAL RELATIONSHIP HANDBOOK *by* KEVIN B. BURK
SERENDIPITY PRESS, FEBRUARY 2006
TRADE PAPERBACK/ISBN 0-9759682-8-9/$19.95 U.S.
6161 EL CAJON BLVD #306, SAN DIEGO CA • www.TheRealAstrology.com/Relationship
CONTACT: KEVIN BURK, 619.807.2473 • KEVIN@EVERYRELATIONSHIP.COM

therealastrology.com
with Kevin B. Burk
Relationship Astrology
Correspondence Course

Yes! You can learn how to use Classical Astrology to reveal key relationship patterns in the natal chart and to understand and improve every relationship in your life!

Study astrology with internationally-acclaimed author and astrologer, Kevin B. Burk!

When most people begin to study astrology, the first thing they want to know is what their birth chart has to say about them. The second thing they want to know is what their birth chart has to say about their relationships.

Now, you can learn the secrets of relationship astrology—including the *only* accurate way to evaluate compatibility—and discover how to use astrology for relationship coaching and counseling!

✔ Listen to live recordings of an actual 12-week class in your web browser.

✔ Download PDF files of all handouts, charts, and assignments—and receive feedback on your homework assignments.

✔ Study at your own pace, in your own time.

Plus, when you register for the course, you will receive...

✔ Access to exclusive video clips and animations that further illustrate key techniques and concepts.

✔ Unlimited eMail support on class topics and assignments.

✔ A total of one hour of one-on-one telephone tutoring with Kevin B. Burk.

✔ A Certificate of Mastery upon successful completion of the final project.

All reading assignments will be from the *Astrological Relationship Handbook* and *The Relationship Handbook* by Kevin B. Burk.

therealastrology.com/classes

www.ingramcontent.com/pod-product-compliance
Ingram Content Group UK Ltd.
Pitfield, Milton Keynes, MK11 3LW, UK
UKHW051300180426
11947UKWH00020B/1818